Mosaic Bla

Beautiful Mosaic Crochet Blanket Patterns

Copyright © 2022

All rights reserved.

DEDICATION

The author and publisher have provided this e-book to you for your personal use only. You may not make this e-book publicly available in any way. Copyright infringement is against the law. If you believe the copy of this e-book you are reading infringes on the author's copyright, please notify the publisher at: https://us.macmillan.com/piracy

Mosaic Blanket

Contents

About Mosaic Crochet 1
Bernat Greek Key Mosaic Crochet Blanket 5
Red Heart Crochet Mosaic Stitch Blanket.............................12
Bernat Party Heart-Y Mosaic Crochet Baby Blanket 21
Red Heart Mosaic Motifs Crochet Blanket 32
Caron Mosaic Motifs Crochet Blanket 45
Caron Interlocking Stitch Crochet Blanket 58
Caron Frenetic Stripes Mosaic Crochet Blanket...................65
Bernat Snow Capped Mosaic Stitch Crochet Blanket 76
Bernat Knit Mosaic Sparkle Baby Blanket 85

About Mosaic Crochet

Is Mosaic Crochet Hard?

Mosaic crochet, despite how complex it looks, only requires a few stitches, two contrasting yarn colors, and some care when it comes to counting. Although it can be used in a variety of garments, its usage in home decor is especially common.

Inset Mosaic Crochet and Overlay Mosaic Crochet – What's the Difference?

There are two types of mosaic crochet techniques: inset and overlay. They produce a similar look and feel but are worked very differently. They both have one thing in common though – each row is worked in a single colour without any changes mid row.

Inset mosaic crochet patterns use two rows per colour giving you an 'a' and 'b' row. In these rows, you create chain spaces that you then work over the top of when you change colour to make it look like they are part of that row.

Closeup of inset mosaic crochet technique.

This means you work lots of US double crochet stitches into the skipped stitches 3 rows below.

This style of mosaic crochet gives a flat and smooth finish and is nice and easy to work back and forth in rows without having to break your yarn.

Mosaic Blanket

In contrast, overlay mosaic crochet patterns use only one row per colour and you will always be working from the right side (RS) of your work. You don't need to create any chain spaces as you do with inset mosaic because you'll always be working into the back loops of your US single crochet stitches, allowing you to work into the front loop only (flo) of the stitches 2 rows below when the chart tells you to.

Mosaic Blanket

This overlay technique is perfect for working in rounds because you can carry your yarn at the back rather than break it. But if you are working in rows, you will have to break your yarn and start the next row on the first stitch of the previous one.

Whether you are looking for mosaic crochet for beginners, or you have several projects under your belt, here's a collection of beautiful patterns from fourteen different designers. Get ready to show off your mosaic crochet skills!

Bernat Greek Key Mosaic Crochet Blanket

Mosaic Blanket

MATERIALS

Bernat® Blanket™ (10.5 oz/300 g; 220 yds/201 m)

Contrast A Cold Sea (04805) 3 balls or 660 yds/603 m

Contrast B Birch (04809) 3 balls or 610 yds/590 m

Size U.S. M/13 (9 mm) crochet hook or size needed to obtain gauge.

ABBREVIATIONS

Approx = Approximately

Beg = Begin(ning)

Ch = Chain(s)

Cont = Continue(ity)

Dc = Double crochet

Mosaic Dc = Working in front of chain spaces, work 1 dc in skipped sc 2 rows below

Rep = Repeat

RS = Right side

Mosaic Blanket

Sc = Single crochet

Sl st = Slip stitch

Sp(s) = Space(s)

St(s) = Stitch(es)

WS = Wrong side

Yoh = Yarn over hook

MEASUREMENTS

Approx 47" x 58" (119.5 x 147.5 cm)

GAUGE

6.5 sc and 7 rows = 4" (10 cm).

INSTRUCTIONS

Notes:

- To change color, work to last loop on hook of previous color. Yoh with new color, draw through loop, tighten previous color and proceed with new color.
- Carry color when not in use loosely up side of work.

Mosaic Blanket

- Each skipped sc has ch-2 worked above it for 2 rows. This establishes the 'gap' where Mosaic Dc will later be worked
- Mosaic Dc always replaces sc directly behind it on working row
- WS of your work maintains alternating 2-row striped pattern because you are working in front of chain spaces each time you work Mosaic Dc - you are never working around chain-spaces. The chain-spaces sit behind Mosaic Dc.
- Blanket worked over foundation ch multiple of 4 ch. With A, ch 80. 1st row: (RS). 1 sc in 2nd ch from hook. 1 sc in each ch to end of chain. Turn. 79 sc. 2nd row: Ch 1. 1 sc in each sc to end of row. Join B. Turn.

Proceed in Mosaic Pat as follows:

1st row: (RS). With B, ch 1. 1 sc in each of rst 3 sc. *Ch 2. Skip next sc. 1 sc in each of next 3 sc. Rep from * to end of row. Turn.

2nd row: Ch 1. 1 sc in each of rst 3 sc. *Ch 2. Skip next 2 ch. 1 sc in each of next 3 sc. Rep from * to end of row. Join A. Turn.

3rd row: With A, ch 1. 1 sc in each of rst 2 sc. *Ch 2. Skip next sc. Mosaic Dc in skipped sc 2 rows below. Ch 2. Skip next sc. 1 sc in next sc. Rep from * to last sc. 1 sc in last sc. Turn.

Mosaic Blanket

4th row: Ch 1. 1 sc in each of first 2 sc. *Ch 2. Skip next 2 ch. 1 sc in next st. Rep from * to last sc. 1 sc in last sc. Join B. Turn.

5th row: With B, ch 1. 1 sc in first sc. Ch 2. Skip next sc. *1 Mosaic Dc in skipped sc 2 rows below. 1 sc in next sc. 1 Mosaic Dc in skipped sc 2 rows below. Ch 2. Skip next sc. Rep from * to last sc. 1 sc in last sc. Turn.

6th row: Ch 1. 1 sc in first sc. Ch 2. Skip next 2 ch. *1 sc in each of next 3 sts. Ch 2. Skip next 2 ch. Rep from * to last sc. 1 sc in last sc. Join A. Turn.

7th row: With A, ch 1. 1 sc in first sc. *1 Mosaic Dc in skipped sc 2 rows below. 1 sc in each of next 3 sc. Rep from * to last 2 sts. 1 Mosaic Dc in skipped sc 2 rows below. 1 sc in last sc. Turn.

8th row: Ch 1. 1 sc in each st to end of row. Join B. Turn.

9th and 10th rows: With B, ch 1. 1 sc in each sc to end of row. Join A. Turn.

11th and 12th rows: With A, as 1st and 2nd rows.

13th and 14th rows: With B, as 3rd and 4th rows.

Mosaic Blanket

15th and 16th rows: With A, as 5th and 6th rows.

17th and 18th rows: With B, as 7th and 8th rows.

19th and 20th rows: With A, ch 1. 1 sc in each sc to end of row. Join B. Turn. Rep these 20 rows for Mosaic Pat until work from beg measures approx 58" [147.5 cm], ending on a 20th row of pat. Do not fasten off. Cont as follows for Side Edging:

Mosaic Blanket

Side Edging:

1st row: (RS). With A, work 1 row of sc evenly down left side edge of Blanket. Turn.

2nd row: Ch 1. 1 sc in each sc to end of row. Fasten o- . With RS facing, join A with sl st in bottom right corner and work as for opposite side edging

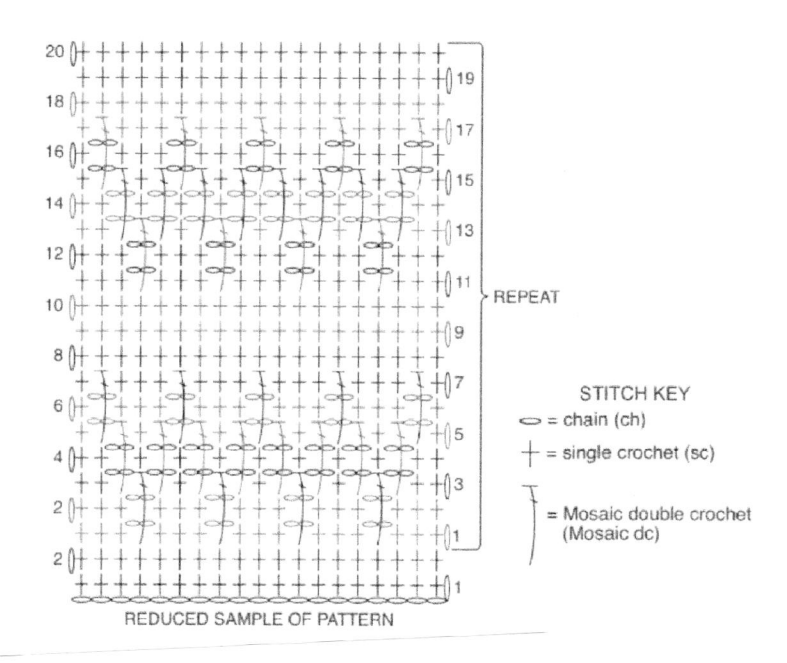

REPEAT

STITCH KEY
◯ = chain (ch)
+ = single crochet (sc)

= Mosaic double crochet (Mosaic dc)

REDUCED SAMPLE OF PATTERN

Red Heart Crochet Mosaic Stitch Blanket

Mosaic Blanket

MATERIALS

Red Heart® Super Saver® (7 oz/198 g; 364 yds/333 m)

Contrast A Oatmeal (0326) 3 balls or 805 yds/730 m

Contrast B Grey Heather (0400) 3 balls or 780 yds/710 m

Contrast C Charcoal (3950) 4 balls or 1295 yds/1175 m

Size U.S. I/9 (5.5 mm) crochet hook or size needed to obtain gauge.

Yarn needle.

ABBREVIATIONS

Approx = Approximately

Beg = Beginning

Ch = Chain(s)

Dc = Double crochet

Hdcfp = Yoh and draw up a loop around post of next stitch at front of work, inserting hook from right to left. Yoh and draw through all loops on hook

Mosaic Blanket

Hdc = Half double crochet

Mosaic Dc = Working in front of chain spaces, work 1 dc in skipped sc 3 rows below

Pat = Pattern

Rem = Remaining

Rep = Repeat

RS = Right side

Sc = Single crochet

Sl st = Slip stitch

Sp(s) = Space(s)

St(s) = Stitch(es)

Tog = Together

Yoh = Yarn over hook

MEASUREMENTS

Approx 50" x 60" [127 x 152.5 cm],

excluding fringe

GAUGE

12 sc and 15 rows = 4" [10 cm]

INSTRUCTIONS

Notes:

- To change color, work to last loop on hook of previous color. Yoh with new color, draw through loop, tighten previous color and proceed with new color.
- Carry color when not in use loosely up side of work unless otherwise stated.
- Each skipped sc has ch-1 worked above it for 2 rows. This establishes the 'gap' where Mosaic Dc will later be worked.
- Mosaic Dc always replaces sc directly behind it on working row
- WS of your work maintains alternating 2-row striped pattern because you are working in front of chain spaces each time you work Mosaic Dc - you are never working around chain-spaces. The chain-spaces are positioned behind Mosaic Dc.
- Ch 3 at beg of row counts as dc.

Mosaic Blanket

- Ch 2 at beg of row does not count as stitch.

With C, ch 151 (multiple of 12 ch + 7).

Foundation row: (WS). 1 sc in 2nd ch from hook and each ch to end of chain. Turn. 150 sc.

**Proceed in Stripe Pat as follows:

1st row: (RS). With C, ch 3. 1 dc in each sc to end of row. Turn.

2nd row: Ch 1. 1 sc in each dc to end of row. Turn.

3rd and 4th rows: As 1st and 2nd rows.

5th and 6th rows: With B, as 1st and 2nd rows.

Rep 1st to 6th rows once more.

Next row: (RS). With C, ch 2. 1 hdc in each sc to end of row. Turn.

Next row: Ch 1. 1 sc in first hdc. 1 hdcfp around each st to last hdc. 1 sc in last hdc.

Next 2 rows: Ch 1. 1 sc in each of first 2 sts. *1 sc in each of next 6 sc. Ch 2. Skip next 2 sc. 1 sc in each of next 4 sc. Rep from * to last 4 sts. 1 sc in each of last 4 sc. Turn. Join A.

Mosaic Blanket

Proceed in Mosaic Pat as follows:

1st row: (RS). With A, ch 1. 1 sc in each of first 2 sc. *1 sc in each of next 4 sc. Ch 2. Skip next 2 sc. Mosaic Dc in each of next 2 skipped sc 3 rows below. Ch 2. Skip next 2 sc. 1 sc in each of next 2 sc. Rep from * to last 4 sts. 1 sc in each of last 4 sc. Turn.

2nd row: Ch 1. 1 sc in each of first 2 sc. *1 sc in each of next 4 sc. Ch 2. Skip next 2 ch. 1 sc in each of next 2 dc. Ch 2. Skip next 2 ch. 1 sc in each of next 2 sc. Rep from * to last 4 sts. 1 sc in each of last 4 sc. Turn.

3rd row: With C, ch 1. 1 sc in each of first 2 sc. *1 sc in each of next 2 sc. Ch 2. Skip next 2 sc. Mosaic Dc in each of next 2 skipped sc 3 rows below. 1 sc in each of next 2 sc. Mosaic Dc in each of next 2 skipped sc 3 rows below. Ch 2. Skip next 2 sc. Rep from * to last 4 sts. 1 sc in each of last 4 sc. Turn.

4th row: Ch 1. 1 sc in each of first 2 sc. *1 sc in each of next 2 sc. Ch 2. Skip next 2 ch. 1 sc in each of next 6 sts. Ch 2. Skip next 2 ch. Rep from * to last 4 sts. 1 sc in each of last 4 sc. Turn.

5th row: With A, ch 1. 1 sc in each of first 2 sc. *Ch 2. Skip next 2 sc.

Mosaic Blanket

Mosaic Dc in each of next 2 skipped sc 3 rows below. 1 sc in each of next 6 sc. Mosaic Dc in each of next 2 skipped sc 3 rows below. Rep from * to last 4 sc. Ch 2. Skip next 2 sc. 1 sc in each of last 2 sc. Turn.

6th row: Ch 1. 1 sc in each of first 2 sc. *Ch 2. Skip next 2 ch. 1 sc in each of next 10 sts. Rep from * to last 4 sts. Ch 2. Skip next 2 ch. 1 sc in each of last 2 sc. Turn.

7th row: With C, ch 1. 1 sc in each of first 2 sc. *Mosaic Dc in each of next 2 skipped sc 3 rows below. 1 sc in each of next 4 sc. Ch 2. Skip next 2 sc. 1 sc in each of next 4 sc. Rep from * to last 4 sts. Mosaic Dc in each of next 2 skipped sc 3 rows below. 1 sc in each of last 2 sc. Turn.

8th row: Ch 1. 1 sc in each of first 2 sc. *1 sc in each of next 6 sts. Ch 2. Skip next 2 ch. 1 sc in each of next 4 sc. Rep from * to last 4 sts. 1 sc in each of last 4 sts. Turn.

Rep these 8 rows for Mosaic Pat 3 times more.

Proceed as follows:

1st row: (RS). With A, ch 1. 1 sc in each of first 2 sc. *1 sc in each of next 6 sc. Mosaic Dc in each of next 2 skipped sc 3 rows below. 1 sc in each of next 4 sc. Rep from * to last 4 sts. 1 sc in each of last 4 sc. Turn.

2nd row: Ch 1. 1 sc in each st to end of row. Turn. Join B.

3rd row: (RS). With B, ch 2. 1 hdc in each sc to end of row. Turn.

4th row: Ch 1. 1 sc in first hdc. 1 hdcfp around each st to last hdc. 1 sc in last hdc. Turn.

Proceed in Stripe Pat as follows:

1st row: With B, ch 3. 1 dc in each st to end of row. Turn.

2nd row: Ch 1. 1 sc in each dc to end of row. Turn.

3rd and 4th rows: With C, as 1st and 2nd rows.

5th to 8th rows: With B, as 1st and 2nd rows twice.

9th and 10th rows: With C, as 1st and 2nd rows.

11th and 12th rows: With B, as 1st and 2nd rows.**

Rep from ** to ** twice more, substituting C for A at end of Mosaic Pat at center section. Fasten off.

Finishing

Mosaic Blanket

Pin Blanket to measurements on a flat surface. Cover with a damp cloth leaving cloth to dry.

Side edging: With RS facing, join C with sl st to top left corner. Work 1 row of sc evenly across side edge of Blanket. Fasten off.

Rep for other side.

Fringe: Cut strands of A, B and C 16" [40.5 cm] long. Taking 1 strand each of A, B and C tog, fold in half and knot into fringe across both ends of Blanket. Trim fringe evenly.

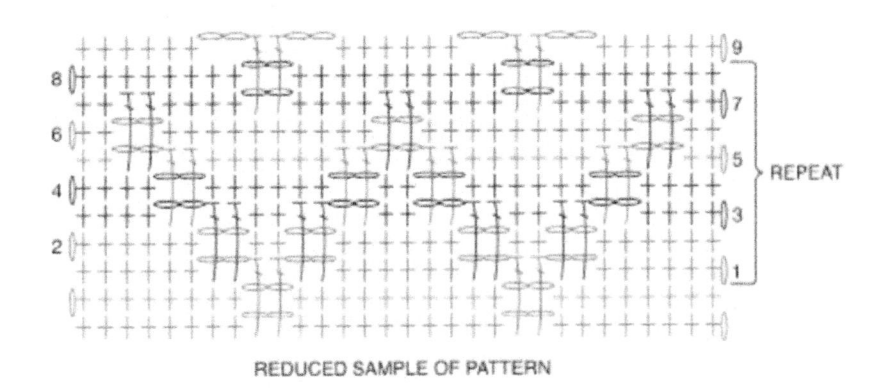

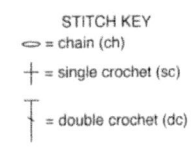

REDUCED SAMPLE OF PATTERN

STITCH KEY
◯ = chain (ch)
+ = single crochet (sc)
= double crochet (dc)

Bernat Party Heart-Y Mosaic Crochet Baby Blanket

MATERIALS

Bernat® Baby Velvet™ (10.5 oz/300 g; 492 yds/450 m)

Contrast A Indigo Velvet (86035) 1 ball

Contrast B Tropical Aqua (86046) 1 ball

Contrast C Bleached Aqua (86030) 1 ball

Contrast D Coral (86048) 1 ball

Mosaic Blanket

Contrast E Flannel (86049) 1 ball

Size U.S. H/8 (5 mm) crochet hook or size needed to obtain gauge

ABBREVIATIONS

Approx = Approximately

Beg = Begin(ning)

Ch = Chain(s)

Mosaic dc = Working in front of previous rows, 1 dc in skipped sc 3 rows below. Skip next ch-2 space (behind mosaic dc).

Pat = Pattern

Rep = Repeat

RS = Right side

Sc = Single crochet

Sl st = Slip stitch

Sp = Space

St(s) = Stitch(es)

Mosaic Blanket

Yoh = Yarn over hook

MEASUREMENT

Approx 40" [101.5 cm] square.

GAUGE

13 sc and 14 rows = 4" [10 cm].

INSTRUCTIONS

Notes:

- To change colors, work to last 2 loops on hook of previous stitch and draw new color through.
- When working Mosaic Heart Pat, carry color not in use loosely up side of work, keeping color change to WS.

With A, ch 114 (multiple of 18 ch + 6).

Foundation row: (WS). 1 sc in 2nd ch from hook. 1 sc in each ch to end of chain. Turn. 113 sc.

With A as color 1 and D as color 2, beg Mosaic Heart Pat as follows:

1st row: With Color 1, ch 1. 1 sc in each of rst 2 sc. *1 sc in each of next 5 sc. Ch 2. Skip next sc. 1 sc in each of next 7 sc. Ch 2. Skip next sc. 1 sc in each of next 4 sc. Rep from * to last 3 sc. 1 sc in each of last 3 sc. Turn.

2nd row: With Color 1, ch 1. 1 sc in each of rst 3 sc. *1 sc in each of next 4 sc. Ch 2. Skip next ch-2 sp. 1 sc in each of next 7 sc. Ch 2. Skip next ch-2 sp. 1 sc in each of next 5 sc. Rep from * to last 2 sc. 1 sc in each of last 2 sc. Turn.

3rd row: With Color 2, ch 1. 1 sc in each of rst 2 sc. *1 sc in each of next 5 sc. Mosaic dc. Ch 2. Skip next sc. 1 sc in each of next 5 sc. Ch 2. Skip next sc. Mosaic dc. 1 sc in each of next 4 sc. Rep from * to last 3 sc. 1 sc in each of last 3 sc. Turn.

4th row: With Color 2, ch 1. 1 sc in each of rst 3 sc. *1 sc in each of next 5 sts. Ch 2. Skip next ch-2 sp. 1 sc in each of next 5 sc. Ch 2. Skip next ch-2 sp. 1 sc in each of next 6 sts. Rep from * to last 2 sc. 1 sc in each of last 2 sc. Turn.

5th row: With Color 1, ch 1. 1 sc in each of next 2 sc. *1 sc in each of next 2 sc. Ch 2. Skip next sc. 1 sc in each of next 3 sc. Mosaic dc. Ch 2. Skip next sc. 1 sc in each of next 3 sc. Ch 2. Skip next sc. Mosaic dc. 1 sc in each of next 3 sc. Ch 2. Skip next sc. 1 sc in next sc. Rep from

Mosaic Blanket

* to last 3 sc. 1 sc in each of last 3 sc. Turn.

6th row: With Color 1, ch 1. 1 sc in each of next 3 sc. *1 sc in each of next sc. Ch 2. Skip next ch-2 sp. 1 sc in each of next 4 sts. Ch 2. Skip next ch-2 sp. 1 sc in each of next 3 sc. Ch 2. Skip next ch-2 sp. 1 sc in each of next 4 sts. Ch 2. Skip next ch-2 sp. 1 sc in each of next sc. Rep from * to last 3 sc. 1 sc in each of last 3 sc. Turn.

7th row: With Color 2, ch 1. 1 sc in each of rst 2 sc.* 1 sc in each of next 2 sc. Mosaic dc. Ch 2. Skip next sc. (1 sc in each of next 3 sc. Mosaic dc) twice. 1 sc in each of next 3 sc. Ch 2. Skip next sc. Mosaic dc. 1 sc in next sc. Rep from * to last 3 sc. 1 sc in each of last 3 sc. Turn.

8th row: With Color 2, ch 1. 1 sc in each of rst 3 sc.* 1 sc in each of next 2 sts. Ch 2. Skip next ch-2 sp. 1 sc in each of next 11 sts sc. Ch 2. Skip next ch-2 sp.1 sc in each of next 3 sts. Rep from * to last 2 sc. 1 sc in each of last 2 sc. Turn.

9th row: With Color 1, ch 1. 1 sc in each of rst 2 sc. *Ch 2. Skip next sc. 1 sc in each of next 2 sc. Mosaic dc. Ch 2. Skip next sc. 1 sc in each of next 9 sc. Ch 2. Skip next sc. Mosaic dc. 1 sc in each of next 2 sc. Rep from * to last 3 sc. Ch 2. Skip next sc. 1 sc in each of last 2 sc.

Mosaic Blanket

Turn.

10th row: With Color 1, ch 1. 1 sc in each of rst 2 sc. Ch 2. Skip next ch-2 sp. *1 sc in each of next 3 sc. Ch 2. Skip next ch-2 sp. 1 sc in each of next 9 sc. Ch 2. Skip next ch-2 sp. 1 sc in each of next 3 sts. Ch 2. Skip next ch-2 sp. Rep from * to last 2 sc. 1 sc in each of last 2 sc. Turn.

11th row: With Color 2, ch 1. 1 sc in each of rst 2 sc. Mosaic dc. *Ch 2. Skip next sc. 1 sc in each of next 2 sc. Mosaic dc. 1 sc in each of next 9 sc. Mosaic dc. 1 sc in each of next 2 sc. Ch 2. Skip next sc. Mosaic dc. Rep from * to last 2 sc. 1 sc in each of last 2 sc. Turn.

12th row: With Color 2, ch 1. 1 sc in each of rst 3 sts. *Ch 2. Skip next ch-2 sp. 1 sc in each of next 15 sts. Ch 2. Skip next ch-2 sp. 1 sc in next st. Rep from * to last 2 sc. 1 sc in each of last 2 sc. Turn.

13th row: With Color 1, ch 1. 1 sc in each of rst 2 sc. *Ch 2. Skip next sc. Mosaic dc. Ch 2. Skip next sc. 1 sc in each of next 13 sc. Ch 2. Skip next sc. Mosaic dc. Rep from * to last 3 sc. Ch 2. Skip next sc. 1 sc in each of last 2 sc. Turn.

14th row: With Color 1, Ch 1. 1 sc in each of rst 2 sc. Ch 2. Skip next ch-2 sp. *1 sc in next st. Ch 2. Skip next ch-2 sp. 1 sc in each of next 13 sc. Ch 2. Skip next ch-2 sp. 1 sc in next st. Ch 2. Skip next ch-2 sp. Rep from * to last 2 sc. 1 sc in each of last 2 sc. Turn.

15th row: With Color 2, ch 1. 1 sc in each of rst 2 sc. Mosaic dc. *Ch 2. Skip next sc. Mosaic dc. 1 sc in each of next 13 sc. Mosaic dc. Ch 2. Skip next sc. Mosaic dc. Rep from * to last 2 sc. 1 sc in each of last 2 sc. Turn.

16th row: With Color 2, ch 1. 1 sc in each of rst 3 sts. *Ch 2. Skip next ch-2 sp. 1 sc in each of next 15 sts. Ch 2. Skip next ch-2 sp. 1 sc in next sc. Rep from * to last 2 sc. 1 sc in each of last 2 sc. Turn.

17th row: With Color 1, ch 1. 1 sc in each of rst 2 sc. *Ch 2. Skip next sc. Mosaic dc. (1 sc in each of next 2 sc. Ch 2. Skip next st) twice. 1 sc in each of next 3 sc. (Ch 2. Skip next sc. 1 sc in each of next 2 sc) twice. Mosaic dc. Rep from * to last 3 sc. Ch 2. Skip next sc. 1 sc in each of next 2 sc. Turn.

18th row: With Color 1, ch 1. 1 sc in each of rst 2 sc. Ch 2. Skip next ch-2 sp. *(1 sc in each of next 3 sts. Ch 2. Skip next ch-2 sp. 1 sc in each of next 2 sc. Ch 2. Skip next ch-2 sp) twice. 1 sc in each of next 3 sts. Ch 2. Skip next ch-2 sp. Rep from * to last 2 sc. 1 sc in each of

Mosaic Blanket

last 2 sc.

19th row: With Color 2, ch 1. 1 sc in each of rst 2 sts. *Mosaic dc. 1 sc in each of next 2 sc. Ch 2. Skip next sc. Mosaic dc. 1 sc in each of next 2 sc. Mosaic dc. Ch 2. Skip next sc. 1 sc in next sc. Ch 2. Skip next sc. Mosaic dc. 1 sc in each of next 2 sc. Mosaic dc. Ch 2. Skip next sc. 1 sc in each of next 2 sc. Rep from * to last ch-2 sp. Mosaic dc. 1 sc in each of last 2 sc. Turn.

20th row: With Color 2, ch 1. 1 sc in each of rst 3 sts. *1 sc in each of next 2 sc. Ch 2. Skip next ch-2 sp. 1 sc in each of next 4 sts. Ch 2. Skip next ch-2 sp. 1 sc in next sc. Ch 2. Skip next ch-2 sp. 1 sc in each of next 4 sts. Ch 2. Skip next ch-2 sp. 1 sc in each of next 3 sts. Rep from * to last 2 sc. 1 sc in each of last 2 sc. Turn.

21st row: With Color 1, ch-1. 1 sc in each of rst 2 sc. *1 sc in each of next 2 sc. (Ch 2. Skip next sc. Mosaic dc. 1 sc in each of next 4 sc. Mosaic dc) twice. Ch 2. Skip next sc. 1 sc in next sc. Rep from * to last 3 sc. 1 sc in each of last 3 sc. Turn.

22nd row: With Color 1, ch 1. 1 sc in each of rst 3 sc. *1 sc in next

Mosaic Blanket

sc. Ch 2. Skip next ch-2 sp. (1 sc in each of next 6 sts. Ch 2. Skip next ch-2 sp) twice. 1 sc in each of next 2 sc. Rep from * to last 2 sc. 1 sc in each of last 2 sc. Turn.

23rd row: With Color 2, ch 1. 1 sc in each of rst 2 sc. *1 sc in each of next 2 sc. Mosaic dc. (1 sc in each of next 6 sc. Mosaic dc) twice. 1 sc in next sc. Rep from * to last 3 sc. 1 sc in each of last 3 sc. Turn.

24th row: With Color 2, ch 1. 1 sc in each st to end of row. Turn. These 24 rows form Mosaic Heart Pat.

Rep these 24 rows 4 times more in the following color combinations:

B as Color 1, E as Color 2.

C as Color 1, A as Color 2.

D as Color 1, B as Color 2.

E as Color 1, C as Color 2.

Border

With RS facing, join B with sl st to top right corner of Blanket.

1st rnd: With B, ch 1. Work sc evenly around Blanket working 3 sc in

Mosaic Blanket

each corner. Join with sl st to rst sc.

2nd rnd: Ch 1. 1 sc in each sc around, working 3 sc in each corner. Join with sl st to rst sc.

3rd and 4th rnds: With C, as 2nd rnd.

5th and 6th rnds: With D, as 2nd rnd.

7th and 8th rnds: With E, as 2nd rnd.

9th and 10th rnds: with A, as 2nd rnd. Fasten off.

How to read Mosaic Chart:

- Each square of chart represents 1 stitch.
- Right side rows (odd numbered rows) are read from right to left. Wrong side rows (even numbered rows) are read from left to right.
- Each row is worked in one color only. First stitch of chart indicates the color to be used in that row.
- When a contrast color appears (eg: white square in a gray row) work as "ch-2. Skip next st".
- On right side rows when a ch-2 sp appears, work Mosaic dc into

Mosaic Blanket

skipped st 3 rows below.

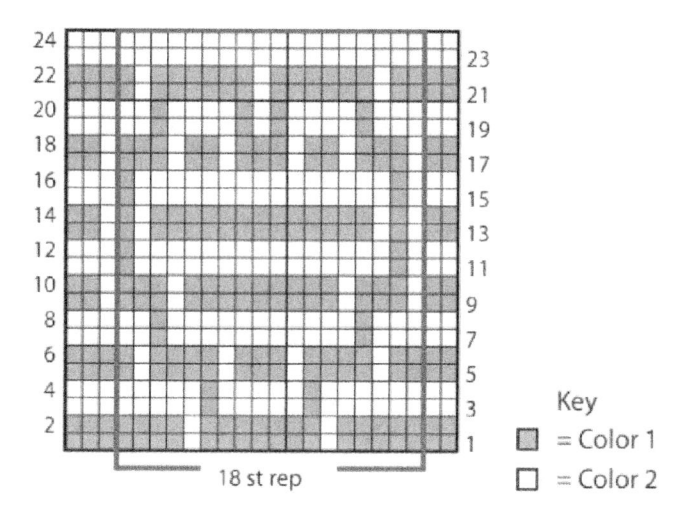

Key
☐ = Color 1
☐ = Color 2

18 st rep

Red Heart Mosaic Motifs Crochet Blanket

Mosaic Blanket

MATERIALS

Red Heart® Super Saver™ (Solids: 7 oz/198 g; 364 yds/333 m)

Contrast A Charcoal (3950) 6 balls

Red Heart® Super Saver™ Ombres (10 oz/283 g; 482 yds/440 m)

Contrast B Sea Coral Ombre (3967) 4 balls

Size U.S. I/9 (5.5 mm) crochet hook or size needed to obtain gauge.

Yarn needle.

ABBREVIATIONS

Approx = Approximately

Ch = Chain(s)

Dc = Double crochet

Hdc = Half double crochet

Mosaic Dc = Working in front of chain space; work 1 dc in next skipped sc 3 rows below. Skip ch-2 space (behind mosaic dc).

Mosaic Blanket

Pat = Pattern

Rem = Remaining

Rep = Repeat

RS = Right side

Sc = Single crochet

Sl st = Slip stitch

Sp(s) = Space(s)

St(s) = Stitch(es)

Tog = Together

WS = Wrong side

MEASUREMENT

Approx 62" [158 cm] square.

GAUGES

11.5 sc and 12 rows = 4" [10 cm]. Motif = 13" [33 cm] square.

Mosaic Blanket

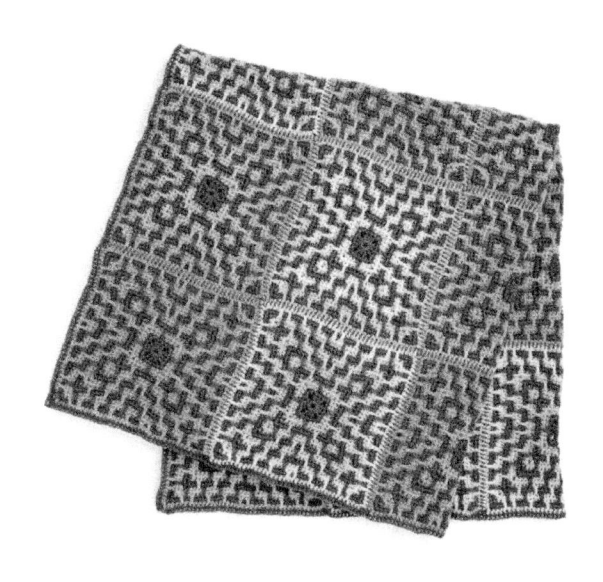

INSTRUCTIONS

Notes:

- To change color, work to last 2 loops on hook and draw new color through last 2 loops, then proceed in new color.
- Each Motif is worked with 2 colors.
- When working Mosaic Dc in rows 3 rows below, work in front of ch-2 spaces, not around.
- Each skipped sc has ch-2 worked above it for 2 rows. This

establishes the 'gap' where Mosaic Dc will later be worked.
- Mosaic Dc always replaces sc directly behind it on working row.
- WS of your work maintains alternating 2-row striped pattern because you are working in front of chain spaces each time you work Mosaic Dc - you are never working around chain-spaces. The chain-spaces are positioned behind Mosaic Dc.

Motif (make 25)

With A, ch 4. Join with sl st to form a ring. (See diagram on page 4).

1st rnd: Ch 3 (counts as dc). 2 dc in ring. (Ch 2. 3 dc) 3 times in ring. Join with 1 hdc in top of first dc. 12 dc.

2nd rnd: Ch 1. 1 sc around post of joining hdc. 1 sc in same sp as joining hdc. 1 sc in each of next 2 dc. *(1 sc. Ch 2. 1 sc) in next ch-2 sp. 1 sc in each of next 3 dc. Rep from * around. 1 sc around post of joining hdc. Join with 1 hdc in top of first sc. Join B. Do not break A.

3rd rnd: With B, ch 1. 1 sc around post of joining hdc. 1 sc in same sp as joining hdc. 1 sc in next sc. *Ch 2. Skip next sc. 1 sc in each of next 2 sc.** (1 sc. Ch 2. 1 sc) in next ch-2 sp. 1 sc in each of next 2 sc. Rep from * twice more, then from * to ** once. 1 sc around post of joining

Mosaic Blanket

hdc. Join with 1 hdc in top of first sc.

4th rnd: Ch 1. 1 sc around post of joining hdc. 1 sc in same sp as joining hdc. 1 sc in each of next 2 sc. *Ch 2. Skip next ch-2 sp. 1 sc in each of next 3 sc.** (1 sc. Ch 2. 1 sc) in next ch-2 sp. 1 sc in each of next 3 sc. Rep from * twice more, then from * to ** once. 1 sc around post of joining hdc. Join with 1 hdc in top of first sc. Join A.

5th rnd: With A, ch 1. 1 sc around post of joining hdc. 1 sc in same sp as joining hdc. *Ch 2. Skip next st. 1 sc in each of next 2 sc. Working in front of B, Mosaic Dc. Skip next ch-2 sp. 1 sc in each of next 2 sc. Ch 2. Skip next sc. 1 sc in next sc.** (1 sc. Ch 2. 1 sc) in next ch-2 sp. 1 sc in next sc. Rep from * twice more, then from * to ** once. 1 sc around post of joining hdc. Join with 1 hdc in top of first sc.

6th rnd: Ch 1. 1 sc around post of joining hdc. 1 sc in same sp as joining hdc. 1 sc in next sc. *Ch 2. Skip next ch-2 sp. 1 sc in each of next 5 sts. Ch 2. Skip next ch-2 sp. 1 sc in each of next 2 sc.** (1 sc. Ch 2. 1 sc) in next ch-2 sp. 1 sc in each of next 2 sc. Rep from * twice more, then from * to ** once. 1 sc around post of joining hdc. Join with 1 hdc in top of first sc. Join B.

7th rnd: With Color 2, ch 1. 1 sc around post of joining hdc. Ch 2.

Mosaic Blanket

Skip first sc. 1 sc in each of next 2 sc. [*Working in front of Color 1, Mosaic Dc. Skip next ch-2 sp. Ch 2. Skip next sc. 1 sc in each of next 3 sc. Ch 2. Skip next sc. Working in front of A, Mosaic Dc. Skip next ch-2 sp. 1 sc in each of next 2 sc. Ch 2. Skip next sc.** (1 sc. Ch 2. 1 sc) in next ch-2 sp. Ch 2. Skip next sc. 1 sc in each of next 2 sc] 3 times. Rep from * to ** to end of rnd. 1 sc around post of joining hdc. Join with 1 hdc in top of first sc.

8th rnd: Ch 1. 1 sc around post of joining hdc. 1 sc in same sp as joining hdc. [*Ch 2. Skip next ch-2 sp. 1 sc in each of next 3 sts. Rep from * to last ch-2 sp and sc before corner ch-2 sp. Ch 2. Skip next ch-2 sp.1sc in next sc.** (1 sc. Ch 2. 1 sc) in corner ch-2 sp. 1 sc in next sc] 3 times. Rep from * to ** to end of rnd. 1 sc around post of joining hdc. Join with 1 hdc in top of first sc. Join A.

9th rnd: With A, ch 1. 1 sc around post of joining hdc. 1 sc in same sp as joining hdc. 1 sc in next sc. [*Working in front of B, Mosaic Dc. Skip next ch-2 sp. Ch 2. Skip next sc. 1 sc in each of next 2 sts. Working in front of Color 2, Mosaic Dc. Skip next ch-2 sp. Ch 2. Skip next sc. 1 sc in next sc. (Ch 2. Skip next sc. Working in front of B, Mosaic Dc. Skip next ch-2 sp. 1 sc in each of next 2 sts) twice. 1 sc in each of next

Mosaic Blanket

2 sc.**(1sc. Ch 2. 1 sc) in corner ch-2 sp. 1 sc in each of next 2 sc] 3 times. Rep from * to ** to end of rnd. 1 sc around post of joining hdc. Join with 1 hdc in top of first sc.

10th rnd: Ch 1. 1 sc around post of joining hdc. 1 sc in same sp as joining hdc. 1 sc in each of next 3 sts. [*(Ch 2. Skip next ch-2 sp. 1 sc in each of next 3 sts. Ch 2. Skip next ch-2 sp. 1 sc in next sc) twice. 1 sc in each of next 3 sc.** (1 sc. Ch 2. 1 sc) in next ch-2 sp. 1 sc in each of next 4 sts] 3 times. Rep from * to ** to end of rnd. 1 sc around post of joining hdc. Join with 1 hdc in top of first sc. Join B.

11th rnd: With B, ch 1. 1 sc around post of joining hdc. 1 sc in same sp as joining hdc. 1 sc in next sc. [*(Ch 2. Skip next sc. 1 sc in each of next 2 sc. Working in front of Color 1, Mosaic Dc. Skip next ch-2 sp) twice. Ch 2. Skip next sc. (Working in front of A, Mosaic Dc. Skip next ch-2 sp. 1 sc in each of next 2 sts. Ch 2. Skip next sc) twice. 1 sc in each of next 2 sc.** (1 sc. Ch 2. 1 sc) in next ch-2 sp. 1 sc in each of next 2 sc] 3 times. Rep from * to ** to end of rnd. 1 sc around post of joining hdc. Join with 1 hdc in top of first sc.

12th rnd: Ch 1. 1 sc around post of joining hdc. 1 sc in same sp as joining hdc. 1 sc in each of next 2 sc. [*Ch 2. Skip next ch-2 sp. 1 sc in each of next 3 sts. Rep from * to corner ch-2 sp.** (1 sc. Ch 2. 1 sc) in next ch-2 sp. 1 sc in each of next 3 sc] 3 times. Rep from * to ** to end of rnd. 1 sc around post of joining hdc. Join with 1 hdc in top of first sc. Join A.

13th rnd: With A, ch 1. 1 sc around post of joining hdc. 1 sc in same sp as joining hdc. [Ch 2. Skip next sc. *(1 sc in each of next 2 sc. Working in front of Color 2, Mosaic Dc. Skip next ch-2 sp. Ch 2. Skip next sc) twice. 1 sc in each of next 2 sc. Working in front of B, Mosaic Dc. Skip next ch-2 sp. 1 sc in each of next 2 sc. (Ch 2. Skip next sc. Working in front of B, Mosaic Dc. Skip next ch-2 sp. 1 sc in each of next 2 sc) twice. Ch 2. Skip next sc. 1 sc in next sc.** (1 sc. Ch 2. 1 sc) in next ch-2 sp. 1 sc in next sc] 3 times. Rep from * to ** to end of rnd. 1 sc around post of joining hdc. Join with 1 hdc in top of first sc.

14th rnd: Ch 1. 1 sc around post of joining hdc. 1 sc in same sp as joining hdc. 1 sc in next sc. [*(Ch 2. Skip next ch-2 sp. 1 sc in each of next 3 sts) twice. Ch 2. Skip next ch-2 sp. 1 sc in each of next 5 sts. (Ch 2. Skip next ch-2 sp. 1 sc in each of next 3 sts) twice. Ch 2. Skip next ch-2 sp. 1 sc in each of next 2 sts.** (1 sc. Ch 2. 1 sc) in next ch-2 sp.1sc in each of next 2 sc] 3 times. Rep from * to ** to end of rnd.

Mosaic Blanket

1 sc around post of joining hdc. Join with 1 hdc in top of first sc. Join B.

15th rnd: With B, ch 1. 1 sc around post of joining hdc. [*(Ch 2. Skip next sc. 1 sc in each of next 2 sc. Working in front of A, Mosaic Dc. Skip next ch-2 sp) 3 times. Ch 2. Skip next sc. 1 sc in each of next 3 sc. (Ch 2. Skip next sc. Working in front of A, Mosaic Dc. Skip next ch-2 sp. 1 sc in each of next 2 sc) 3 times. Ch 2. Skip next sc.** (1 sc. Ch 2. 1 sc) in next ch-2 sp] 3 times. Rep from * to ** to end of rnd. 1 sc around post of joining hdc. Join with 1 hdc in top of first sc.

16th rnd: Ch 1. 1 sc around post of joining hdc. 1 sc in same sp as joining hdc. [*(Ch 2. Skip next ch-2 sp. 1 sc in each of next 3 sts) 7 times. Ch 2. Skip next ch-2 sp. 1 sc in next sc.** (1 sc. Ch 2. 1 sc) in next ch-2 sp. 1 sc in next sc] 3 times. Rep from * to ** to end of rnd. 1 sc around post of joining hdc. Join with 1 hdc in top of first sc. Join A.

17th rnd: With A, ch 1. 1 sc around post of joining hdc. 1 sc in same sp as joining hdc. [*Ch 2. Skip next sc. (Working in front of B, Mosaic Dc. Skip next ch-2 sp. Ch 2. Skip next sc. 1 sc in each of next 2 sc) 3 times. Working in front of B, Mosaic Dc. Skip next ch-2 sp. Ch 2. Skip next sc. 1 sc in next sc. (Ch 2. Skip next sc. Working in front of Color 2, Mosaic Dc. Skip next ch-2 sp. 1 sc in each of next 2 sts) 3 times. Ch 2. Skip next sc. Working in front of B, Mosaic Dc. Skip next ch-2 sp. Ch 2. Skip next sc. 1 sc in next sc.** (1 sc. Ch 2. 1 sc) in next ch-2 sp. 1 sc in next sc] 3 times. Rep from * to ** to end of rnd. 1 sc around post of joining hdc. Join with 1 hdc in top of first sc.

18th rnd: Ch 1. 1 sc around post of joining hdc. 1 sc in same sp as joinng hdc. 1 sc in next sc. [*Ch 2. Skip next ch-2 sp. 1 sc in next st. (Ch 2. Skip next ch-2 sp. 1 sc in each of next 3 sts) 3 times. Ch 2. Skip next ch-2 sp. 1 sc in next sc. (Ch 2. Skip next ch-2 sp. 1 sc in each of next 3 sts) 3 times. (Ch 2. Skip next ch-2 sp. 1 sc in next st) twice. 1 sc in next sc.** (1 sc. Ch 2. 1 sc) in next ch-2 sp. 1 sc in next sc] 3 times. Rep from * to ** to end of rnd. 1 sc around post of joining hdc. Join with 1 hdc in top of first sc. Join B.

19th rnd: With B, ch 1. 1 sc around post of joining hdc. 1 sc in same sp as joining hdc. 1 sc in each of next 2 sc. [*Working in front of A, Mosaic Dc. Skip next ch-2 sp. 1 sc in next sc. (Working in front of A, Mosaic Dc. Skip next ch-2 sp.1 sc in each of next 3 sts) 3 times. Rep from * once more. Working in front of A, Mosaic Dc. Skip next ch-2

Mosaic Blanket

sp. 1 sc in next sc. Working in front of A, Mosaic Dc. Skip next ch-2 sp. 1 sc in each of next 3 sc.**(1 sc. Ch 2. 1 sc) in next ch-2 sp. 1 sc in each of next 3 sc] 3 times. Rep from * to ** to end of rnd. 1 sc around post of joining hdc. Ch 2. Join with sl st to first sc. Fasten off.

Finishing

Join Motifs tog with sc into 5 Strips and 5 Motifs into each Strip as follows:

With RS facing each other, join A with sl st to corner ch-2 sp. Working through both thicknesses, work 1 sc in each st to next ch-2 sp. Fasten off. Join 5 Strips into Blanket as follows: With RS facing each other, join A with sl st to corner ch-2 sp. Working through both thicknesses, work in sc across Strip to next corner ch-2 sp. Fasten off.

Border

With RS facing, join A with sl st to any ch-2 sp corner.

1st rnd: Ch 2 (does not count as st). 2 hdc in same sp as sl st. 1 hdc in each st around, working (2 hdc. Ch 2. 2 hdc) in ch-2 sp corners. Join B with hdc in top of first hdc.

Mosaic Blanket

2nd and 3rd rnds: With B, ch 2. 2 hdc around post of joining hdc. 1 hdc in same sp as joining hdc and each hdc around, working (2 hdc. Ch 2. 2 hdc) in ch-2 sp corners. Join with hdc in top of first hdc.

4th rnd: Ch 1. Working from left to right, instead of from right to left, as usual, work 1 reverse sc in each sc around. Join with sl st to first sc. Fasten off.

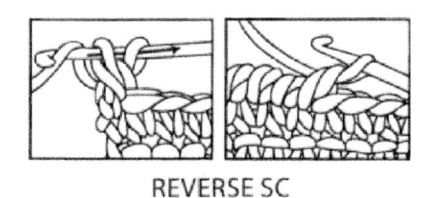

REVERSE SC

Corner ch-2 sp

Beg of rnd

Note: Only ¼ of Motif is shown. Rem 3 sections of Motif will repeat this Diagram

Key
☐ = Contrast A
☐ = Contrast B
⌒ = ch
⊤ = dc
+ = sc
= 1 dc in next sc 3 rows below
⌒ = Joining hdc

Caron Mosaic Motifs Crochet Blanket

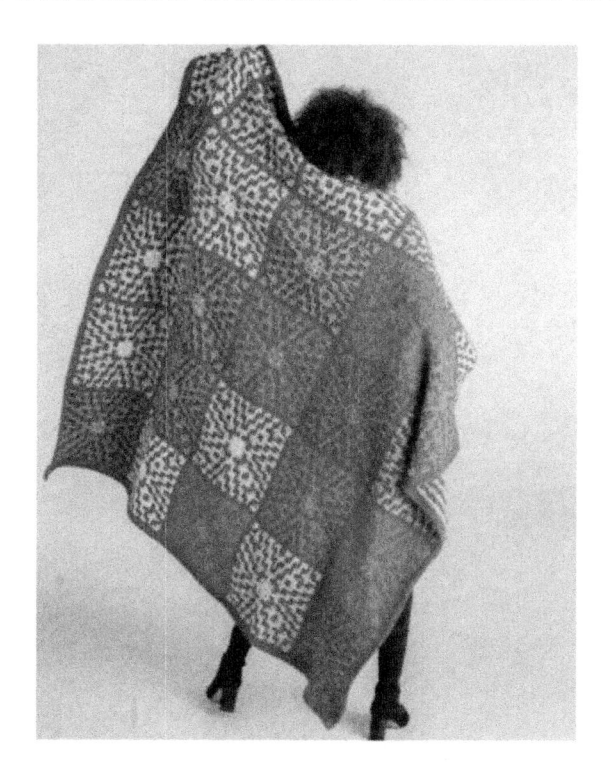

MATERIALS

Caron® Big Donut™ O'Go™ (9.9 oz/280 g; 502 yds/459 m)

Main Color (MC) Fireberry (29012) 4 O'Gos

Contrast I Mint Julep (29008) 2 O'Gos

Mosaic Blanket

Contrast II Raspberry Glazed (29006) 2 O'Gos

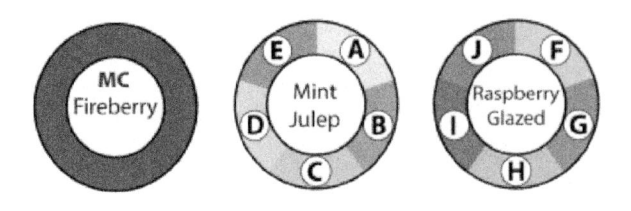

Size U.S. I/9 (5.5 mm) crochet hook or size needed to obtain gauge.

Yarn needle.

ABBREVIATIONS

Approx = Approximately

Ch = Chain(s)

Dc = Double crochet

Hdc = Half double crochet

Mosaic Dc = Working in front of chain spaces, work 1 dc in skipped sc 3 rows below

Pat = Pattern

Rem = Remaining

Mosaic Blanket

Rep = Repeat

Rnd(s) = Round(s)

RS = Right side

Sc = Single crochet

Sl st = Slip stitch

Sp(s) = Space(s)

St(s) = Stitch(es)

Tog = Together

WS = Wrong side

MEASUREMENT

Approx 62" [158 cm] square.

GAUGES

12.5 sc and 13 rows = 4" [10 cm]. 1 Motif = 12" [30.5 cm] square.

INSTRUCTIONS

Notes:

Mosaic Blanket

- To begin working with the O'Go format, carefully cut plastic tie where the ends of the O'Go meet.
- Pull tie to remove.
- For this pattern, colors can be easily separated by gently pulling apart and cutting at the color transition. Each color is ready to use. Follow color guide shown in Materials section for each O'Go (Contrast A through J). You may find it helpful to place each color section in its own resealable (zip lock) bag and label each bag A through J.
- To change color, work to last 2 loops on hook and draw new color through last 2 loops, then proceed in new color.
- Each Motif is worked with 2 colors only.
- When working dc in rows 3 rows below, work in front of ch-2 spaces, not around.
- Each skipped sc has ch-2 worked above it for 2 rows. This establishes the 'gap' where Mosaic Dc will later be worked
- Mosaic Dc always replaces sc directly behind it on working row
- WS of your work maintains alternating 2-row striped pattern because you are working in front of chain spaces each time you work Mosaic Dc - you are never working around chain-spaces.

Mosaic Blanket

The chain-spaces are positioned behind Mosaic Dc.

MOTIFS

Make 2 with A as Color 1 and MC as Color 2.

Make 2 with B as Color 1 and MC as Color 2.

Make 2 with C as Color 1 and MC as Color 2.

Make 3 with D as Color 1 and MC as Color 2.

Make 3 with E as Color 1 and MC as Color 2.

Make 3 with F as Color 1 and MC as Color 2.

Make 3 with G as Color 1 and MC as Color 2.

Make 2 with H as Color 1 and MC as Color 2.

Make 3 with I as Color 1 and MC as Color 2.

Make 2 with J as Color 1 and MC as Color 2.

MOTIF INSTRUCTIONS

With Color 1, ch 4. Join with sl st to form a ring. (See diagram on page 5).

Mosaic Blanket

1st rnd: Ch 3 (counts as dc). 2 dc in ring. (Ch 2. 3 dc) 3 times in ring. Join with 1 hdc in top of first dc. 12 dc.

2nd rnd: Ch 1. 1 sc around post of joining hdc. 1 sc in same sp as joining hdc. 1 sc in each of next 2 dc. * (1 sc. Ch 2. 1 sc) in next ch-2 sp. 1 sc in each of next 3 dc. Rep from * around. 1 sc around post of joining hdc. Join with 1 hdc in top of first sc. Join Color 2, Do not break Color 1.

3rd rnd: With Color 2, ch 1. 1 sc around post of joining hdc. 1 sc in same sp as joining hdc. 1 sc in next sc. *Ch 2. Skip next sc. 1 sc in each of next 2 sc.** (1 sc. Ch 2. 1 sc) in next ch-2 sp. 1 sc in each of next 2 sc. Rep from * twice more, then from * to ** once. 1 sc around post of joining hdc. Join with 1 hdc in top of first sc.

4th rnd: Ch 1. 1 sc around post of joining hdc. 1 sc in same sp as joining hdc. 1 sc in each of next 2 sc. *Ch 2. Skip next ch-2 sp. 1 sc in each of next 3 sc.** (1 sc. Ch 2. 1 sc) in next ch-2 sp. 1 sc in each of next 3 sc. Rep from * twice more, then from * to ** once. 1 sc around post of joining hdc. Join with 1 hdc in top of first sc. Join Color 1,

5th rnd: With Color 1, ch 1. 1 sc around post of joining hdc. 1 sc in same sp as joining hdc. *Ch 2. Skip next st. 1 sc in each of next 2 sc.

Mosaic Blanket

Working in front of Color 2, Mosaic Dc. Skip next ch-2 sp. 1 sc in each of next 2 sc. Ch 2. Skip next sc. 1 sc in next sc.** (1 sc. Ch 2. 1 sc) in next ch-2 sp. 1 sc in next sc. Rep from * twice more, them from * to ** once. 1 sc around post of joining hdc. Join with 1 hdc in top of first sc.

6th rnd: Ch 1. 1 sc around post of joining hdc. 1 sc in same sp as joining hdc. 1 sc in next sc. *Ch 2. Skip next ch-2 sp. 1 sc in each of next 5 sts. Ch 2. Skip next ch-2 sp. 1 sc in each of next 2 sc.** (1 sc. Ch 2. 1 sc) in next ch-2 sp. 1 sc in each of next 2 sc. Rep from * twice more, then from * to ** once. 1 sc around post of joining hdc. Join with 1 hdc in top of first sc. Join Color 2,

7th rnd: With Color 2, ch 1. 1 sc around post of joining hdc. Ch 2. Skip first sc. 1 sc in each of next 2 sc. [*Working in front of Color 1, Mosaic Dc. Skip next ch-2 sp. Ch 2. Skip next sc. 1 sc in each of next 3 sc. Ch 2. Skip next sc. Working in front of Color 1, Mosaic Dc. Skip next ch-2 sp. 1 sc in each of next 2 sc. Ch 2. Skip next sc.** (1 sc. Ch 2. 1 sc) in next ch-2 sp. Ch 2. Skip next sc. 1 sc in each of next 2 sc.] 3 times. Rep from * to ** to end of rnd. 1 sc around post of joining hdc. Join with 1 hdc in top of first sc.

Mosaic Blanket

8th rnd: Ch 1. 1 sc around post of joining hdc. 1 sc in same sp as joining hdc. [*Ch 2. Skip next ch-2 sp. 1 sc in each of next 3 sts. Rep from * to last ch-2 sp and sc before corner ch-2 sp. Ch 2. Skip next ch-2 sp. 1 sc in next sc.** (1 sc. Ch 2. 1 sc) in corner ch-2 sp. 1 sc in next sc] 3 times. Rep from * to ** 1 sc around post of joining hdc. Join with 1 hdc in top of first sc. Join Color 1.

9th rnd: With Color 1, ch 1. 1 sc around post of joining hdc. 1 sc in same sp as joining hdc. 1 sc in next sc. [*Working in front of Color 2, Mosaic Dc. Skip next ch-2 sp. Ch 2. Skip next sc. 1 sc in each of next 2 sts. Working in front of Color 2, Mosaic Dc. Skip next ch-2 sp. Ch 2. Skip next sc. 1 sc in next sc. (Ch 2. Skip next sc. Working in front of Color 2, Mosaic Dc. Skip next ch-2 sp. 1 sc in each of next 2 sts) twice. 1 sc in each of next 2 sc.** (1 sc. Ch 2. 1 sc) in corner ch-2 sp. 1 sc in each of next 2 sc] 3 times. Rep from * to **. 1 sc around post of joining hdc. Join with 1 hdc in top of first sc.

10th rnd: Ch 1. 1 sc around post of joining hdc. 1 sc in same sp as joining hdc. 1 sc in each of next 3 sts. [*(Ch 2. Skip next ch-2 sp. 1 sc in each of next 3 sts. Ch 2. Skip next ch-2 sp. 1 sc in next sc) twice. 1 sc in each of next 3 sc.** (1 sc. Ch 2. 1 sc) in next ch-2 sp. 1 sc in each

Mosaic Blanket

of next 4 sts] 3 times. Rep from * to ** to end of rnd. 1 sc around post of joining hdc. Join with 1 hdc in top of first sc. Join Color 2.

11th rnd: With Color 2, ch 1. 1 sc around post of joining hdc. 1 sc in same sp as joining hdc. 1 sc in next sc. [*(Ch 2. Skip next sc. 1 sc in each of next 2 sc. Working in front of Color 1, Mosaic Dc. Skip next ch-2 sp) twice. Ch 2. Skip next sc. (Working in front of Color 1, Mosaic Dc. Skip next ch-2 sp. 1 sc in each of next 2 sts. Ch 2. Skip next sc) twice. 1 sc in each of next 2 sc.** (1 sc. Ch 2. 1 sc) in next ch-2 sp. 1 sc in each of next 2 sc] 3 times. Rep from * to ** to end of row. 1 sc around post of joining hdc. Join with 1 hdc in top of first sc.

12th rnd: Ch 1. 1 sc around post of joining hdc. 1 sc in same sp as joining hdc. 1 sc in each of next 2 sc. [*Ch 2. Skip next ch-2 sp. 1 sc in each of next 3 sts. Rep from * to corner ch-2 sp.** (1 sc. Ch 2. 1 sc) in next ch-2 sp. 1 sc in each of next 3 sc] 3 times. Rep from * to ** to end of rnd. 1 sc around post of joining hdc. Join with 1 hdc in top of first sc. Join Color 1.

13th rnd: With Color 1, ch 1. 1 sc around post of joining hdc. 1 sc in same sp as joining hdc. [Ch 2. Skip next sc. *(1 sc in each of next 2 sc. Working in front of Color 2, Mosaic Dc. Skip next ch-2 sp. Ch 2. Skip next sc) twice. 1 sc in each of next 2 sc. Working in front of Color 2, Mosaic Dc. Skip next ch-2 sp. 1 sc in each of next 2 sc. (Ch 2. Skip next sc. Working in front of Color 2, Mosaic Dc. Skip next ch-2 sp. 1 sc in each of next 2 sc) twice. Ch 2. Skip next sc. 1 sc in next sc.** (1 sc. Ch 2. 1 sc) in next ch-2 sp. 1 sc in next sc] 3 times. Rep from * to **. 1 sc around post of joining hdc. Join with 1 hdc in top of first sc.

14th rnd: Ch 1. 1 sc around post of joining hdc. 1 sc in same sp as joining hdc. 1 sc in next sc. [*(Ch 2. Skip next ch-2 sp. 1 sc in each of next 3 sts) twice. Ch 2. Skip next ch-2 sp. 1 sc in each of next 5 sts. (Ch 2. Skip next ch-2 sp. 1 sc in each of next 3 sts) twice. Ch 2. Skip next ch-2 sp. 1 sc in each of next 2 sts.** (1 sc. Ch 2. 1 sc) in next ch-2 sp. 1 sc in each of next 2 sc] 3 times. Rep from * to **. 1 sc around post of joining hdc. Join with 1 hdc in top of first sc. Join Color 2.

15th rnd: With Color 2, ch 1. 1 sc around post of joining hdc. [*(Ch 2. Skip next sc. 1 sc in each of next 2 sc. Working in front of Color 1, Mosaic Dc. Skip next ch-2 sp) 3 times. Ch 2. Skip next sc. 1 sc in each of next 3 sc. (Ch 2. Skip next sc. Working in front of Color 1, Mosaic Dc. Skip next ch-2 sp. 1 sc in each of next 2 sc) 3 times. Ch 2. Skip next sc.** (1 sc. Ch 2. 1 sc) in next ch-2 sp] 3 times. Rep from * to **.

1 sc around post of joining hdc. Join with 1 hdc in top of first sc.

16th rnd: Ch 1. 1 sc around post of joining hdc. 1 sc in same sp as joining hdc. [*(Ch 2. Skip next ch-2 sp. 1 sc in each of next 3 sts) 7 times. Ch 2. Skip next ch-2 sp.. 1 sc in next sc.** (1 sc. Ch 2. 1 sc) in next ch-2 sp. 1 sc in next sc] 3 times. Rep from * to **. 1 sc around post of joining hdc. Join with 1 hdc in top of first sc. Join Color 1.

17th rnd: With Color 1, ch 1. 1 sc around post of joining hdc. 1 sc in same sp as joining hdc. [*Ch 2. Skip next sc. (Working in front of Color 2, Mosaic Dc. Skip next ch-2 sp. Ch 2. Skip next sc. 1 sc in each of next 2 sc) 3 times. Working in front of Color 2, Mosaic Dc. Skip next ch-2 sp. Ch 2. Skip next sc. 1 sc in next sc. (Ch 2. Skip next sc. Working in front of Color 2, Mosaic Dc. Skip next ch-2 sp. 1 sc in each of next 2 sts) 3 times. Ch 2. Skip next sc. Working in front of Color 2, Mosaic Dc. Skip next ch-2 sp. Ch 2. Skip next sc. 1 sc in next sc.** (1 sc. Ch 2. 1 sc) in next ch-2 sp. 1 sc in next sc] 3 times. Rep from * to **. 1 sc around post of joining hdc. Join with 1 hdc in top of first sc.

18th rnd: Ch 1. 1 sc around post of joining hdc. 1 sc in same sp as joining hdc. 1 sc in next sc. [*Ch 2. Skip next ch-2 sp. 1 sc in next st. (Ch 2. Skip next ch-2 sp. 1 sc in each of next 3 sts) 3 times. Ch 2. Skip

Mosaic Blanket

next ch-2 sp. 1 sc in next sc. (Ch 2. Skip next ch-2 sp. 1 sc in each of next 3 sts) 3 times. (Ch 2. Skip next ch-2 sp. 1 sc in next st) twice. 1 sc in next sc.** (1 sc. Ch 2. 1 sc) in next ch-2 sp. 1 sc in next sc] 3 times. Rep from * to **. 1 sc around post of joining hdc. Join with 1 hdc in top of first sc. Join Color 2.

19th rnd: With Color 2, ch 1. 1 sc around post of joining hdc. 1 sc in same sp as joining hdc. 1 sc in each of next 2 sc. [*Working in front of Color 1, Mosaic Dc. Skip next ch-2 sp. 1 sc in next sc. (Working in front of Color 1, Mosaic Dc. Skip next ch-2 sp. 1 sc in each of next 3 sts) 3 times. Rep from * once more. Working in front of Color 1, Mosaic Dc. Skip next ch-2 sp. 1 sc in next sc. Working in front of Color 1, Mosaic Dc. Skip next ch-2 sp. 1 sc in each of next 3 sc.** (1 sc. Ch 2. 1 sc) in next ch-2 sp. 1 sc in each of next 3 sc] 3 times. Rep from * to **. 1 sc around post of joining hdc. Ch 2. Join with sl st to first sc. Fasten off.

Finishing

Following Assembly Diagram, join 5 Motifs tog into each Strip as follows:

With RS facing each other, join MC with sl st to corner ch-2 sp.

Mosaic Blanket

Working through both thicknesses, work 1 sc in each st to next ch-2 sp. Fasten off.

Join 5 Strips into Blanket as follows: With RS facing each other, join MC with sl st to corner ch-2 sp. Working through both thicknesses, work evenly in sc across Strip to next corner ch-2 sp. Fasten off.

Border

With RS facing, join MC with sl st to any corner ch-2 sp.

1st rnd: Ch 2 (does not count as st). 2 hdc in same sp as sl st. 1 hdc in each st around, working (2 hdc. Ch 2. 2 hdc) in corner ch-2 sps. Join with hdc in top of first hdc.

2nd and 3rd rnds: Ch 2. 2 hdc around post of joining hdc. 1 hdc in same sp as joining hdc and each hdc around, working (2 hdc. Ch 2. 2 hdc) in corner ch-2 sps. Join with hdc in top of first hdc. Fasten off.

F	G	H	I	J
H	I	J	G	F
F	E	G	D	I
C	D	E	B	A
A	B	C	D	E

ASSEMBLY DIAGRAM

Caron Interlocking Stitch Crochet Blanket

Mosaic Blanket

MATERIALS

Caron® Simply Soft® (6 oz/170.1 g; 315 yds/288 m)

Contrast A Persimmon (39754) 3 balls

Contrast B Off White (39702) 2 balls

Size U.S. I/9 (5.5 mm) crochet hook or size needed to obtain gauge.

ABBREVIATIONS

Approx = Approximately

Ch = Chain(s)

Dc = Double crochet

Pat = Pattern

Rep = Repeat

RS = Right side

Sc = Single crochet

Sl st = Slip stitch

Sp(s) = Space(s)

Mosaic Blanket

WS = Wrong side

MEASUREMENTS

Approx 32 x 38" [81.5 x 96.5 cm].

GAUGE

12 sc and 13 rows = 4" [10 cm].

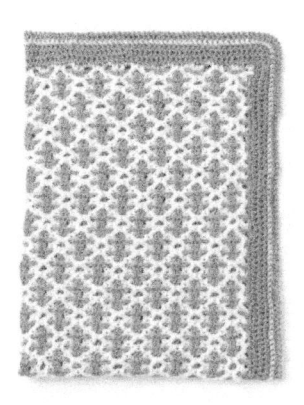

INSTRUCTIONS

Note:

Blanket is reversible. Ch 121 (foundation ch multiple 10 ch + 1).

1st row: (RS). With A, 1 dc in 11th ch from hook (counts as dc and ch

Mosaic Blanket

3 over 4 ch). 1 dc in next ch. *Ch 3. Skip next 3 ch. 1 dc in each of next 2 ch. Rep from * to last 4 ch. Ch 3. Skip next 3 ch. 1 dc in last ch. Do not turn. Pull long loop. Remove hook.

2nd row: (RS). Working in front of A, join B with sl st to 2nd ch. Ch 6 (counts as dc and ch 3). Working behind A, 1 dc in same sp as sl st. *Skip next 2 dc. Working behind A, 1 dc in 2nd ch of next ch-3 sp. Ch 3. Working in front of A, 1 dc in same sp as last dc. Working in front of A, 1 dc in 2nd ch of next ch-3 sp. Ch 3. Working behind A, 1 dc in same sp as last dc. Rep from * to end of row. Pull long loop. Remove hook. Turn.

3rd row: (WS). Re-insert hook into A loop. Ch 6 (counts as dc and ch 3). *Working in front of B, 1 dc in each of next 2 dc 2 rows below (A row). Ch 3. Working behind B, 1 dc in each of next 2 dc 2 rows below (A row). Ch 3. Rep from * to last turning ch. Skip next 3 ch. Working in front of B, 1 dc in next ch of 1st row. Do not turn. Pull long loop. Remove hook.

4th row: (WS). Re-insert hook into B loop. Ch 3 (counts as dc). Working in front of A, 1 dc in 2nd ch of first ch-3 sp 2 rows below (B row). Ch 3. Working behind A, 1 dc in same sp as last dc. *Working behind A, 1 dc in 2nd ch of next ch-3 sp. Ch 3. Working in front of A, 1 dc in same sp as last dc. Working in front of A, 1 dc in 2nd ch of next ch-3 sp 2 rows below (B row). Ch 3. Working behind A, 1 dc in same sp as last dc. Rep from * to end of row. Pull long loop. Remove hook. Turn.

5th row: (RS). Re-insert hook into A loop. Ch 6 (counts as dc and ch 3). *Working behind B, 1 dc in each of next 2 dc 2 rows below (A row). Ch 3. Working in front of B, 1 dc in each of next 2 dc 2 rows below (A row). Ch 3. Rep from * to last turning ch. Skip next 3 ch. Working behind B, 1 dc in next ch 2 rows below (3rd row). Do not turn. Pull long loop. Remove hook.

6th row: (RS). Re-insert hook into B loop. Ch 3 (counts as dc). Working behind A, 1 dc in 2nd ch of first ch-3 sp 2 rows below (B row). Ch 3. Working in front of A, 1 dc in same sp as last dc. *Working in front of A, 1 dc in 2nd ch of next ch-3 sp. Ch 3. Working behind A, 1 dc in same sp as last dc. Working behind A, 1 dc in 2nd ch of next ch-3 sp 2 rows below (B row). Ch 3. Working in front of A, 1 dc in same sp as last dc. Rep from * to end of row. Pull long loop. Remove hook. Turn.

Mosaic Blanket

7th row: (WS). As 5th row, noting row is WS.

8th row: (WS). Re-insert hook into B loop. Ch 3 (counts as dc). Working behind A, 1 dc in 2nd ch of first ch-3 sp 2 rows below. Ch 3. Working in front of A, 1 dc in same sp as last dc. *Working in front of A, 1 dc in 2nd ch of next ch-2 sp 2 rows below. Ch 3. Working behind A, 1 dc in same sp as last dc. Working behind A, 1 dc in 2nd ch of next ch-2 sp 2 rows below. Ch 3. Working in front of A, 1 dc in same sp as last dc. Rep from * to end of row. Pull long loop. Remove hook. Turn.

9th row: (RS). As 3rd row, noting row is RS.

10th row: (RS). As 4th row, noting row is RS. Rep 3rd to 10th rows for pat until work from beg measures approx 38" [96.5 cm], ending with B row. Fasten off.

Border:

With RS facing, join A with sl st to top right corner of Blanket. Ch 1. Work 96 sc evenly across top of Blanket. 3 sc in corner. Work 114 sc evenly down left side of Blanket. 3 sc in corner. Work 96 sc evenly across bottom of Blanket. 3 sc in corner. Work 114 sc evenly up right side of Blanket. 3 sc in corner. Join with sl st to first sc.

Mosaic Blanket

2nd to 5th rnds: Ch 1. 1 sc in each sc around, working 3 sc in each corner sc. Join with sl st to first sc. Join B at end of 5th rnd. Do not break A.

6th rnd: With B, as 2nd rnd. Join A at end of rnd. Break B.

7th rnd: With A, as 2nd rnd.

8th rnd: Ch 1. Working from left to right, instead of from right to left, as usual, work 1 reverse sc in each sc around. Join with sl st to rst sc. Fasten off.

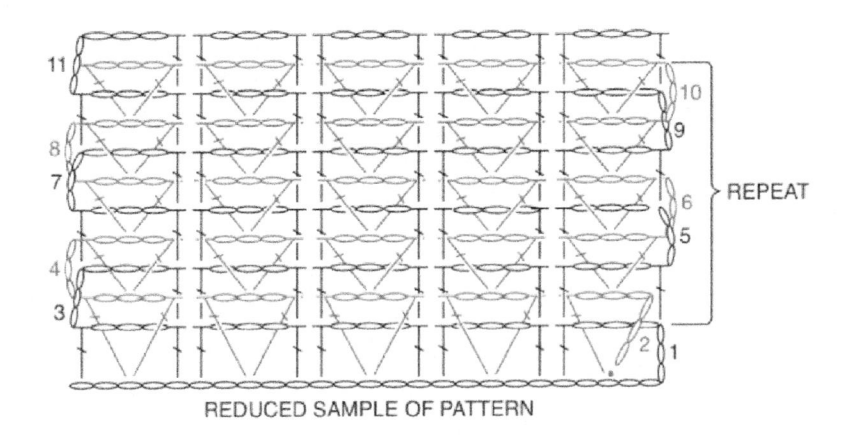

REDUCED SAMPLE OF PATTERN

STITCH KEY
⌒ = chain (ch)
• = slip stitch (sl st)
┬ = double crochet (dc)

Caron Frenetic Stripes Mosaic Crochet Blanket

Mosaic Blanket

MATERIALS

Caron® One Pound™ (16 oz/453.6 g; 812 yds/742 m)

Contrast A White (10501) 2 balls

Contrast B Royalty (10530) 1 ball Contrast C Aqua (10622) 1 ball

Contrast D Ocean (10611) 1 ball Contrast E Off White (10514) 1 ball

Size U.S. J/10 (6 mm) crochet hook or size needed to obtain gauge. Yarn needle.

ABBREVIATIONS

Approx = Approximately

BLO = Back loop only

Ch = Chain(s)

Dc = Double crochet

(Mosaic Dc) twice = Working in front of chain spaces; work 1 dc in each of 2 skipped sc 3 rows below. Skip ch-3 space (behind mosaic dc).

Pat = Pattern

Mosaic Blanket

Rep = Repeat

Rnd(s) = Round(s)

RS = Right side

Sc = Single crochet

Sl st = Slip stitch

Sp(s) = Space(s)

St(s) = Stitch(es)

Tog = Together

WS = Wrong side

MEASUREMENTS

Approx 52" x 59½" [132 x 151 cm], excluding fringe.

GAUGE

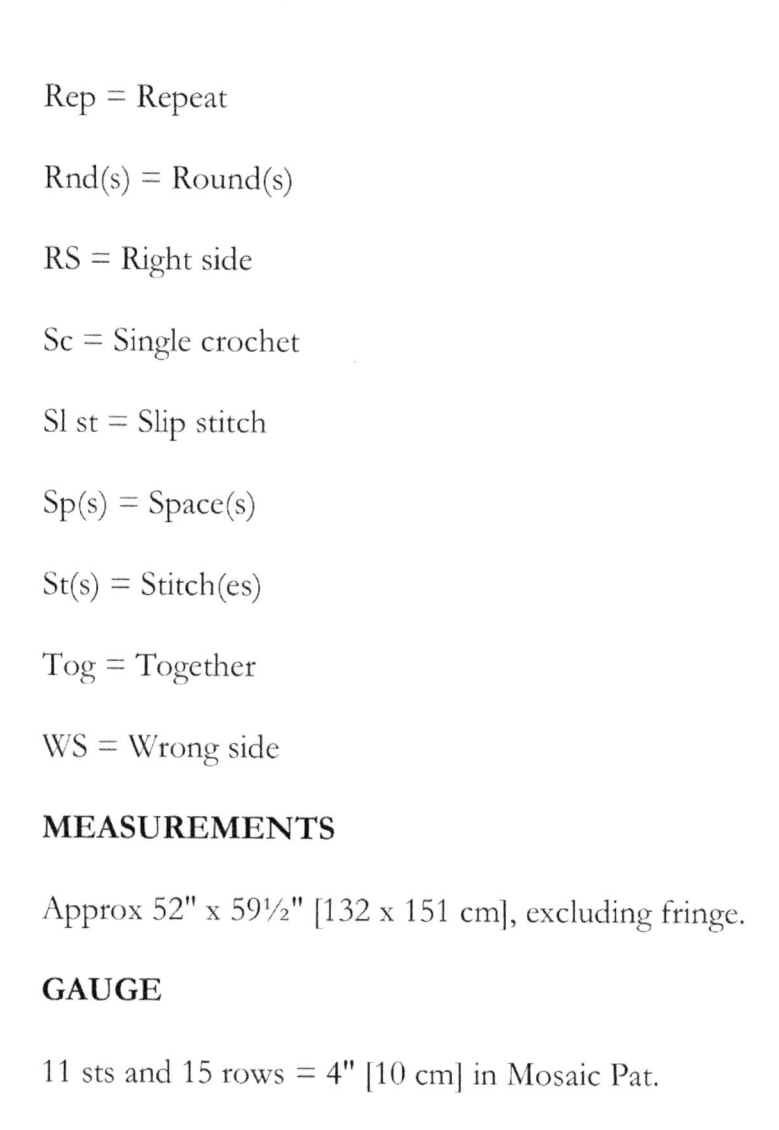

11 sts and 15 rows = 4" [10 cm] in Mosaic Pat.

INSTRUCTIONS

Notes:

Mosaic Blanket

- To change colors, work to last 2 loops on hook of previous stitch and draw new color through.
- When working Mosaic Pat, carry color not in use loosely up side of work unless otherwise stated.
- Each pair of skipped sc has ch-3 worked above it for 2 rows. This establishes the 'gap' where 2 Mosaic Dc will later be worked
- Mosaic Dc always replaces sc directly behind it on working row
- WS of your work maintains alternating 2-row striped pattern because you are working in front of chain spaces each time you work Mosaic Dc - you are never working around chain-spaces. The chain-spaces sit behind Mosaic Dc.
- On RS rows when working into a st that is a different color than current working color, work sts into back loops only. If st you are working into is same color, work under both loops as usual.
- Blanket is worked lengthwise, from side to side.

Blanket

With A, ch 163 (multiple of 8 ch + 11).

Set-up row: (WS). 1 sc in 2nd ch from hook. 1 sc in each ch to end of chain. Turn. 162 sc.

Mosaic Blanket

Proceed with First Mosaic Stripe where Color 1 is A and Color 2 is B as follows:

1st row: (RS). With Color 1, ch 1. 1 sc in each of first 2 sc. *Ch 3. Skip next 2 sc. 1 sc in each of next 6 sc. Rep from * to end of row. Turn.

**2nd row: (WS). With Color 1, ch 1. *1 sc in each of next 6 sc. Ch 3. Skip next ch-3. Rep from * to last 2 sc. 1 sc in each of last 2 sc. Turn.

3rd row: With Color 2, ch 1. Working in BLO, 1 sc in each of first 2 sc. *Working in BLO, (Mosaic Dc) twice. Ch 3. Skip next 2 sc. Working in BLO, 1 sc in each of next 2 sc. Ch 3. Skip next 2 sc. Rep from * to last 8 sts. Working in BLO, (Mosaic Dc) twice. Ch 3. Skip next 2 sc. Working in BLO, 1 sc in each of last 4 sc. Turn.

4th row: With Color 2, ch 1. 1 sc in each of first 4 sc. Ch 3. Skip next ch-3. 1 sc in each of next 2 sts. *Ch 3. Skip next ch-3. 1 sc in each of next 2 sts. Rep from * to last 2 sc. 1 sc in each of last 2 sc. Turn.

5th row: With Color 1, ch 1. Working in BLO, 1 sc in each of first 2 sc. *[Ch 3. Skip next 2 sc. (Mosaic Dc) twice] twice. Rep from * to last 8 sc. Ch 3. Skip next 2 sc. (Mosaic Dc) twice. Ch 3. Skip next 2 sc. Working in BLO, 1 sc in each of last 2 sc. Turn.

Mosaic Blanket

6th row: With Color 1, ch 1. 1 sc in each of first 2 sc. Ch 3. Skip next ch-3. 1 sc in each of next 2 sc. Ch 3. Skip next ch-3 *1 sc in each of next 2 sc. Ch 3. Skip next ch-3. Rep from * to last 2 sc. 1 sc in each of last 2 sc. Turn.

7th row: With Color 2, ch 1. Working in BLO, 1 sc in each of first 2 sc. *(Mosaic Dc) twice. Working in BLO, 1 sc in each of next 2 sc. (Mosaic Dc) twice. Ch 3. Skip next 2 sc. Rep from * to last 8 sts. *(Mosaic Dc) twice. Working in BLO, 1 sc in each of next 2 sc. (Mosaic Dc) twice. Working in BLO, 1 sc in each of last 2 sc. Turn.

8th row: With Color 2, ch 1. 1 sc in each of first 8 sts. *Ch 3. Skip next ch-3. 1 sc in each of next 6 sts. Rep from * to last 2 sc. 1 sc in each of last 2 sc. Turn.

9th row: With Color 1, ch 1. Working in BLO, 1 sc in each of first 2 sc. *Ch 3. Skip next 2 sc. Working in BLO, 1 sc in each of next 2 sc. Ch 3. Skip next 2 sc. (Mosaic Dc) twice. Rep from * to last 8 sts. Ch 3. Skip next 2 sc. Working in BLO, 1 sc in each of next 2 sc. Ch 3. Skip next 2 sc. Working in BLO, 1 sc in each of last 2 sc. Turn.

10th row: With Color 1, ch 1. 1 sc in each of first 2 sts. *Ch 3. Skip next ch-3. 1 sc in each of next 2 sts. Rep from * to end of row. Turn.

Mosaic Blanket

11th row: With Color 2, ch 1. Working in BLO, 1 sc in each of first 2 sc. *(Mosaic Dc) twice. Ch 3. Skip next 2 sc. (Mosaic Dc) twice. Ch 3. Skip next 2 sc. Rep from * to last 8 sts. (Mosaic Dc) twice. Ch 3. Skip next 2 sc. (Mosaic Dc) twice. Working in BLO, 1 sc in each of last 2 sc. Turn.

12th row: With Color 2, ch 1. 1 sc in each of first 4 sc. Ch 3. Skip next ch-3. 1 sc in each of next 2 sts. *Ch 3. Skip next ch-3. 1 sc in each of next 2 sts. Rep from * to last 2 sts. 1 sc in each of last 2 sts. Turn. Join new Color 1 (as below). Break Color 2.**

Mosaic Blanket

Proceed with Mosaic Stripe Pat where Color 1 is C and Color 2 is A as follows:

1st row: (RS). With Color 1, ch 1. Working in BLO, 1 sc in each of first 2 sc. *Ch 3. Skip next 2 sc. Working in BLO, (Mosaic Dc) twice. Working in BLO, 1 sc in each of next 2 sc. Working in BLO, (Mosaic Dc) twice. Rep from * to last 8 sts. Ch 3. Skip next 2 sc. Working in BLO, (Mosaic Dc) twice. Working in BLO, 1 sc in each of last 4 sc. Turn.

2nd to 12th rows: Rep from ** to ** as given for First Mosaic Stripe. These 12 rows form Mosaic Stripe Pat.

Work 12 rows of Mosaic Stripe Pat where Color 1 is D and Color 2 is C.

Work 12 rows of Mosaic Stripe Pat where Color 1 is E and Color 2 is D.

Work 12 rows of Mosaic Stripe Pat where Color 1 is B and Color 2 is E.

*** Work 12 rows of Mosaic Stripe Pat where Color 1 is A and Color 2 is B.

Mosaic Blanket

Work 12 rows of Mosaic Stripe Pat where Color 1 is C and Color 2 is A.

Work 12 rows of Mosaic Stripe Pat where Color 1 is D and Color 2 is C.

Work 12 rows of Mosaic Stripe Pat where Color 1 is E and Color 2 is D.

Work 12 rows of Mosaic Stripe Pat where Color 1 is B and Color 2 is E.

*** Rep from *** to *** once more.

Work 12 rows of Mosaic Stripe Pat where Color 1 is A and Color 2 is B.

Next row: (RS). With A, ch 1. Working in BLO, 1 sc in each of first 2 sc. *Working in BLO, 1 sc in each of next 2 sc. (Mosaic Dc) twice. Rep from * to last 8 sts. Working in BLO, 1 sc in each of next 2 sc. (Mosiac Dc) twice. Working in BLO, 1 sc in each of last 4 sc. Fasten off.

Edging:

1st rnd: (RS). Join A with sl st to any corner of Blanket. Ch 1. Work

Mosaic Blanket

sc evenly around Blanket, working around yarn carried loosely up side of work to enclose it, and working (1 sc. Ch 2. 1 sc) in each corner. Join with sl st to first sc. Fasten off.

Fringe: Cut lengths of A 14" [35.5 cm] long. Taking 3 strands tog, knot into fringe in every other st along top and bottom edges of Blanket (as shown in photo). Trim fringe evenly.

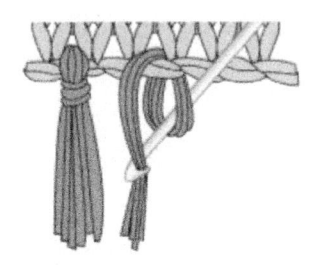

How to read Mosaic Chart:

- Each square of chart represents 1 stitch.
- RS rows (odd numbered rows) are read from right to left. WS rows (even numbered rows) are read from left to right.
- Each row is worked in one color only. First stitch of chart indicates the color to be used in that row.
- When a contrast color appears (eg: 2 white squares in a gray row) work as "ch 3. Skip next 2 sts".

Mosaic Blanket

- On RS rows when working into a st that is a different color than current working color, work sts into back loops only. If working into st of same color, work under both loops as usual.
- On RS rows when a ch-3 sp appears, work 1 Mosaic Dc into each of 2 skipped sts 3 rows below.

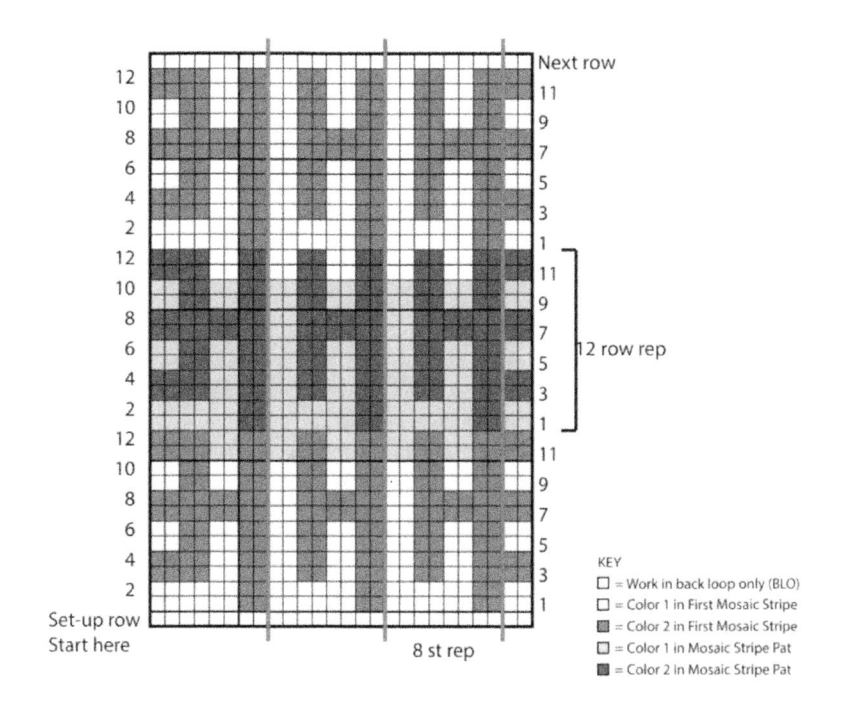

12 row rep

8 st rep

Set-up row
Start here

KEY
☐ = Work in back loop only (BLO)
☐ = Color 1 in First Mosaic Stripe
▨ = Color 2 in First Mosaic Stripe
☐ = Color 1 in Mosaic Stripe Pat
■ = Color 2 in Mosaic Stripe Pat

Bernat Snow Capped Mosaic Stitch Crochet Blanket

MATERIALS

Bernat® Crushed Velvet™ (10.5 oz/300 g; 315 yds/288 m)

Mosaic Blanket

Contrast A Soft Gray (16001) 4 balls or 1021 yds/934 m

Contrast B White (16007) 2 balls or 578 yds/529 m

Bernat® Blanket™ (10.5 oz/300 g; 220 yds/201 m)

Contrast C Vintage White (10006) 2 balls or 351 yds/321 m

Sizes U.S. I/9 (5.5 mm) and U.S. L/11 (8 mm) crochet hooks or sizes needed to obtain gauge. 6" [15 cm] piece of cardboard for tassels. Yarn needle.

ABBREVIATIONS

Approx = Approximately

Ch = Chain(s)

Mosaic Dc = Working in front of chain spaces, work 1 dc in skipped sc 3 rows below

Pat = Pattern

Rep = Repeat

Mosaic Blanket

Rnd(s) = Round(s)

RS = Right side

Sc = Single crochet

Sl st = Slip stitch

St(s) = Stitch(es)

Tr = Treble crochet

WS = Wrong side

Yoh = Yarn over hook

MEASUREMENTS

Approx 50½" [128.5 cm] wide x 55" [139.5 cm] long.

GAUGES

12 sts and 15.5 rows = 4" [10 cm] in Mosaic Pat with smaller hook and Bernat® Crushed Velvet™.

7 sc and 8 rows = 4" [10 cm] with larger hook and Bernat® Blanket™.

INSTRUCTIONS

Mosaic Blanket

Notes:

- To change color, work to last loop on hook of previous color. Yoh with new color, draw through loop, tighten previous color and proceed with new color.
- Carry color when not in use loosely up side of work unless otherwise stated.
- Each skipped sc has ch-1 worked above it for 2 rows. This establishes the 'gap' where Mosaic Dc will later be worked
- Mosaic Dc always replaces sc directly behind it on working row
- WS of your work maintains alternating 2-row striped pattern because you are working in front of chain spaces each time you work Mosaic Dc - you are never working around chain-spaces. The chain-spaces are positioned behind Mosaic Dc.
- Blanket worked over foundation ch multiple of 24 ch +7.

FIRST MOSAIC PANEL

With smaller hook and A, ch 151.

Mosaic Set-up: 1st row: (WS). 1 sc in 2nd ch from hook. 1 sc in each ch to end of chain. Turn. 150 sc.

Mosaic Blanket

**2nd row: Ch 1. 1 sc in each of first 2 sc. *1 sc in each of next 6 sc. Ch 2. Skip next 2 sc. 1 sc in each of next 4 sc. Rep from * to last 4 sc. 1 sc in each of last 4 sc. Turn.

3rd row: Ch 1. 1 sc in each of next 2 sc. *1 sc in each of next 6 sc. Ch 2. Skip next 2 ch. 1 sc in each of next 4 sc. Rep from * to last 4 sc. 1 sc in each of last 4 sc. Turn.

Begin working Mosaic Pat as follows: See diagram on page 3.

1st row: With B, ch 1. 1 sc in each of first 2 sc. *1 sc in each of next 4 sc. Ch 2. Skip next 2 sc. Mosaic Dc in each of next 2 skipped sc 3 rows below. Ch 2. Skip next 2 sc. 1 sc in each of next 2 sc. Rep from * to last 4 sts. 1 sc in each of last 4 sc. Turn.

2nd row: Ch 1. 1 sc in each of first 2 sc. *1 sc in each of next 4 sc. Ch 2. Skip next 2 ch. 1 sc in each of next 2 dc. Ch 2. Skip next 2 ch. 1 sc in each of next 2 sc. Rep from * to last 4 sts. 1 sc in each of last 4 sc. Turn.

3rd row: With A, ch 1. 1 sc in each of first 2 sc. *1 sc in each of next 2 sc. Ch 2. Skip next 2 sc. Mosaic Dc in each of next 2 skipped sc 3 rows below. 1 sc in each of next 2 sc. Mosaic Dc in each of next 2 skipped sc 3 rows below. Ch 2. Skip next 2 sc. Rep from * to last 4 sts. 1 sc in each of last 4 sc. Turn.

4th row: Ch 1. 1 sc in each of first 2 sc. *1 sc in each of next 2 sc. Ch 2. Skip next 2 ch. 1 sc in each of next 6 sts. Ch 2. Skip next 2 ch. Rep from * to last 4 sts. 1 sc in each of last 4 sc. Turn.

5th row: With B, ch 1. 1 sc in each of first 2 sc. *Ch 2. Skip next 2 sc. Mosaic Dc in each of next 2 skipped sc 3 rows below. 1 sc in each of next 6 sc. Mosaic Dc in each of next 2 skipped sc 3 rows below. Rep from * to last 4 sc. Ch 2. Skip next 2 sc. 1 sc in each of last 2 sc. Turn.

6th row: Ch 1. 1 sc in each of first 2 sc. *Ch 2. Skip next 2 ch. 1 sc in each of next 10 sts. Rep from * to last 4 sts. Ch 2. Skip next 2 ch. 1 sc in each of last 2 sc. Turn.

7th row: With A, ch 1. 1 sc in each of first 2 sc. *Mosaic Dc in each of next 2 skipped sc 3 rows below. 1 sc in each of next 4 sc. Ch 2. Skip next 2 sc. 1 sc in each of next 4 sc. Rep from * to last 4 sts. Mosaic Dc in each of next 2 skipped sc 3 rows below. 1 sc in each of last 2 sc. Turn.

8th row: Ch 1. 1 sc in each of first 2 sc. *1 sc in each of next 6 sts. Ch

Mosaic Blanket

2. Skip next 2 ch. 1 sc in each of next 4 sc. Rep from * to last 4 sts. 1 sc in each of last 4 sts. Turn. These 8 rows form Mosaic pat. Rep 1st through 8 rows once more.

Next row: (RS). With A, ch 1. 1 sc in each of first 2 sc. *1 sc in each of next 6 sc. Mosaic Dc in each of next 2 skipped sc 3 rows below. 1 sc in each of next 4 sc. Rep from * to last 4 sc. 1 sc in each of last 4 sc. Turn.

Next row: Ch 1. 1 sc in each st to end of row. Fasten off. Turn.**

BOBBLE STRIPE

Notes:

- Bobble Stripe worked over st multiple of 2 sc +1.
- Push tr sts worked on WS to RS of work to form bobbles.

1st row: (RS). With larger hook, join C with sl st to work across last row. Ch 1. *1 sc in next sc. Skip next sc. 1 sc in next sc. [Skip next sc. 1 sc in each of next 2 sc. (Skip next sc. 1 sc in next sc) twice] 3 times. Rep from * to last 6 sc. (Skip next sc. 1 sc in next sc) 3 times. Turn. 87 sc.

Mosaic Blanket

2nd row: Ch 1. 1 sc in first sc.*1 tr in next sc. 1 sc in next sc. Rep from * to end or row. Turn.

3rd row: Ch 1. 1 sc in each st to end of row. Fasten off. Turn.

SECOND MOSAIC PANEL

Mosaic Set-up:

1st row: (WS). With smaller hook, join A with sl st to work across last row. Ch 1 *2 sc in next sc. 1 sc in next sc. (2 sc in next sc. 1 sc in next sc. 2 sc in each of next 2 sc) 3 times. Rep from * to last 3 sc. 2 sc in each of last 3 sc. Turn. 150 sc. Work from ** to ** as for First Mosaic Panel. Rep Bobble Stripe and Second Mosaic Panel 6 times more. Fasten off.

FINISHING

Edging:

1st rnd: (RS). With larger hook, join C with sl st to any corner of Blanket. Work sc evenly around Blanket, working around yarn carried loosely up side of work to enclose it and working 3 sc in each corner. Join with sl st to first sc. Fasten off.

Mosaic Blanket

Tassels (make 4): Wind C around a piece of cardboard 6" [15 cm] wide 20 times. Tie through loops securely at one end leaving 2 long tails. Cut across other end. Wrap yarn 6 times around Tassel 1½" [4 cm] down from tied end. Fasten securely. Tie 1 Tassel to each corner sc of Blanket using long tails (as shown in photo).

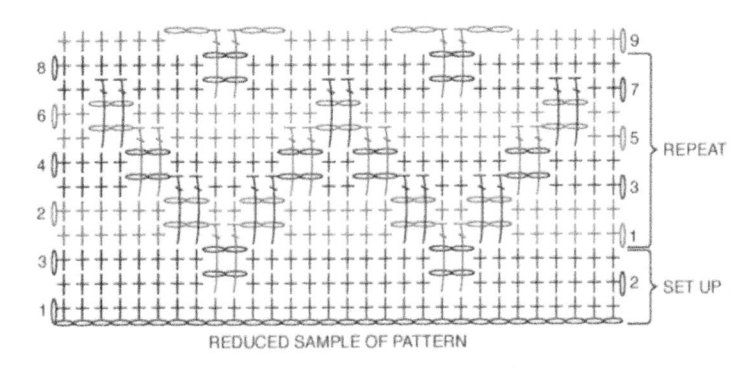

REDUCED SAMPLE OF PATTERN

STITCH KEY
⌒ = chain (ch)
+ = single crochet (sc)
T = double crochet (dc)

Bernat Knit Mosaic Sparkle Baby Blanket

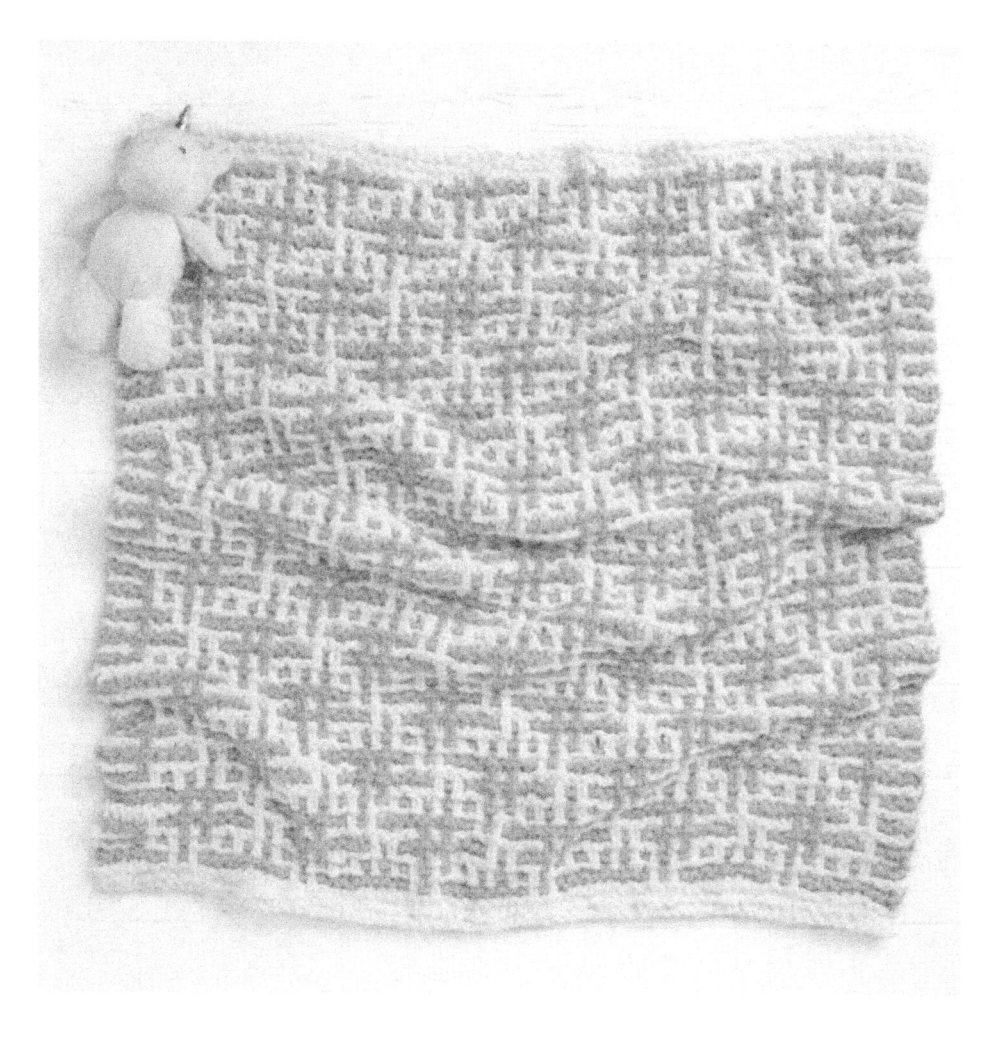

Mosaic Blanket

MATERIALS

Bernat® Baby Blanket Sparkle™ (10.5 oz/300 g; 220 yds/201 m)

Contrast A Moonlight Sparkle (71001) 2 balls or 289 yds/264 m

Contrast B Rose Glow Sparkle (71002) 2 balls or 260 yds/237 m

Size U.S. 11 (8 mm) circular knitting needle 29" [73.5 cm] long or size needed to obtain gauge.

ABBREVIATIONS

Alt = Alternate(ing)

Approx = Approximately

Beg = Begin(ning)

K = Knit

Pat = Pattern

Rep = Repeat

RS = Right side

Sl1Pwyib = Slip next stitch purlwise with yarn in back of work

Mosaic Blanket

Sl1Pwyif = Slip next stitch purlwise with yarn in front of work

St(s) = Stitch(es)

WS = Wrong side

MEASUREMENT

Approx 39" [99 cm] square.

GAUGE

8 sts and 13 rows = 4" [10 cm] in stocking st

INSTRUCTIONS

Notes:

- Every row is worked with 1 color only.

- Carry color not in use loosely along side of work.

BLANKET

With A, cast on 78 sts (multiple of 12 sts + 6). Do not join.

Edging: Working back and forth across needle in rows, knit 3 rows, noting 1st row is WS.

Mosaic Blanket

Proceed in pat as follows:

1st row: (RS). With B, K3. *K6. Sl1Pwyib. K1. Sl1Pwyib. K3. Rep from * to last st. K1.

2nd and alt rows: Using same color as previous row, knit all knit sts and Sl1wyif all slipped sts.

Mosaic Blanket

3rd row: With A, K3. *K1. Sl1Pwyib. K5. Sl1Pwyib. K3. Sl1Pwyib. Rep from * to last 3 sts. K3.

5th row: With B, K3. *Sl1Pwyib. K1. Rep from * to last 3 sts. K3.

7th row: With A, K3. *K5. Sl1Pwyib. K1. Sl1Pwyib. K3. Sl1Pwyib. Rep from * to last 3 sts. K3.

9th row: With B, K3. *Sl1Pwyib. K9. Sl1Pwyib. K1. Rep from * to last 3 sts. K3.

11th row: With A, K3. *K5. Sl1Pwyib. K1. Sl1Pwyib. K4. Rep from * to last 3 sts. K3.

13th row: With B, K3. *Sl1Pwyib. K1. Sl1Pwyib. K9. Rep from * to last 3 sts. K3.

15th row: With A, K3. *K1. Sl1Pwyib. K3. Sl1Pwyib. K1. Sl1Pwyib. K4. Rep from * to last 3 sts. K3.

17th row: As 5th row.

19th row: With A. K3. *K1. Sl1Pwyib. K3. Sl1Pwyib. K5. Sl1Pwyib. Rep from * to last 3 sts. K3.

21st row: With B, K3. *K4. Sl1Pwyib. K1. Sl1Pwyib. K5. Rep from *

Mosaic Blanket

to last 3 sts. K3.

23rd row: With A, K3. *K1. Sl1Pwyib. K9. Sl1Pwyib. Rep from * to last 3 sts. K3.

24th row: As 2nd row.

Rep 1st to 24th rows for pat until work from beg measures approx 39" [99 cm], ending on 12th or 24th row.

Edging: With A, knit 3 rows. Cast off.

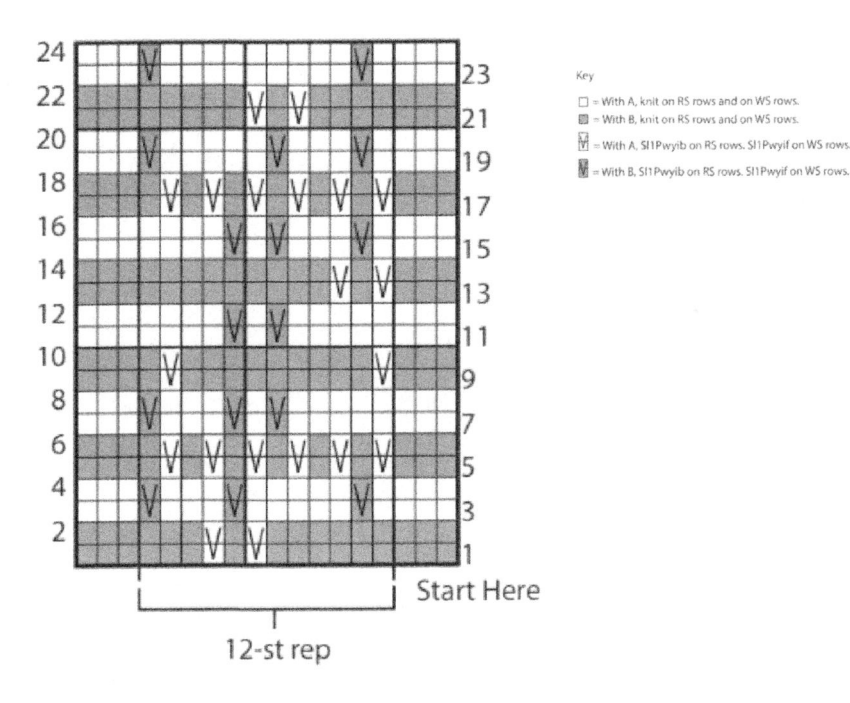

Key
□ = With A, knit on RS rows and on WS rows.
▨ = With B, knit on RS rows and on WS rows.
V = With A, Sl1Pwyib on RS rows. Sl1Pwyif on WS rows.
V = With B, Sl1Pwyib on RS rows. Sl1Pwyif on WS rows.

Start Here

12-st rep

Printed in Great Britain
by Amazon